The Road to Success

Nuensie Suku

with Howard Griffin, Ph.D.

A Small Business Owner's Guide to Life, Financial Freedom, and Achieving Your Dreams

Hope my book will bring you lots of success — Thank you for your support

God Bless

Nuensie Suku

(NANCY)

Library of Congress Cataloging-in-Publication Data
Suku, Nuensie- 1956-
Griffin, Howard- 1973-

Summary: Coming from Thailand, Suku shares life and business philosophies that she crafted through her unique experiences and perspective on life.

Library of Congress Control Number: 2011934326

Designed by *James* (msjamesin@gmail.com)

Printed in the United States of America

Georgia Typeface used in *The Road to Success*

DEDICATION

To my parents, who taught me the value of hard work; my nephew, who inspired me with his ability to bounce back from tragedy; and my family, who supported me through all the difficult times.

DISCLAIMER

Although the events related in this volume are factual, the names of persons mentioned throughout the book have been changed in order to protect their privacy.

TABLE OF CONTENTS

Prologue

I was born in a small village in Isan Province, Thailand, along the border with Laos and Cambodia. Thailand is classified as an emerging economy, but much of the economic growth has only occurred since the early 1990s. Isan Province, where I was born, has traditionally been, and continues to be, one of the poorest regions in the country. It is primarily agricultural and rural in nature. The provincial capital is comprised of around 140,000 people, although it was somewhat smaller when I was a girl. Given our proximity to Laos, we tend to identify more with Laos than the rest of Thailand. The provincial language, also called Isan, is in fact a dialect of the Lao language and is everyone's first language, although most everyone speaks Thai (to a greater or lesser degree). In fact, I speak Isan much better and easier than I speak standard Thai. It's a Buddhist country; some of the primary tenets of Buddhism are ethical living, mindfulness, meditation and the cultivation of wisdom (Padmasambhava et. al, 2004). Although I'm not a strict Buddhist, I think these are some excellent objectives to have for daily living.

The reason I relate to you, my esteemed reader, the above information about my background is to provide you a backdrop for what is to come. I believe that my past has directly influenced my perspective on entrepreneurship.

Everyone has a different take on life-- its purpose, the overall meaning of why we are here, and what we are meant to do. Although it may have taken me a longer time to discover my purpose and special talents in life than for others, I now consider entrepreneurship to be the road that I should travel in this world.

The remainder of this tome will describe in detail to you the means by which I transformed myself into an entrepreneur, the techniques that I have learned over the last seven or eight years, and the unique business philosophy I have crafted for myself during this time as a result of my distinctive circumstances and personality traits. Everyone's experiences are different, and you most assuredly will encounter your own challenges, difficulties, and triumphs as an entrepreneur. My desire is that you find something in this work to inspire you, guide you, and provide you with insight as to what it means to be a small business owner. In my view, it is the ultimate manner in which to be the "master of your own destiny."

Chapter I
Entrepreneurship

Entrepreneurship is the act of undertaking a business endeavor in an effort to transform innovations into economic goods or services. In fact, it comes from the French word meaning, "to undertake an endeavor" (Shane, 2004). It is the cornerstone of the American economy, creates tens of thousands of jobs each year, and is something a large percentage of people worldwide aspire to. In a very basic sense, being an entrepreneur means starting, owning, and operating one's own business. Entrepreneurs are for the most part well respected and admired.

Many people associate having one's own business with undertaking a large amount of risk-- the fear if the business goes under, the business owner will lose everything. Although it is true that only a fraction of businesses ever reach their fifth birthday, there are ways the business owner can protect himself or herself. Most entrepreneurs that operate a company of any significant size will be incorporated (there are many different forms of incorporation, but the basic principles are the same). This means if the business does go under, the business owner will only be "on the hook" for the liabilities that were a part of the corporation. In other words, creditors could only potentially come after the assets held within the corporation-- nothing more. Thus, a corporate structure offers protection to the business owner's personal assets (home, cars, retirement funds, and other assets) in this scenario.

Additionally, and perhaps counterintuitively, the business owner actually runs less risk than a salaried employee does. The salaried employee has only one stream of income-- the current employer. If the employer fires or lets the employee go for whatever reason, the employee must find another job-- something that is not easy to do in today's economy. The business owner, on the other hand, has hundreds, if not thousands, of sources of income-- the individual customers that he or she has and the potential customers the business owner could gain in the future through advertising, word-of-mouth or other means. Thus, the business owner has less risk of "getting fired" in the sense if one customer stops patronizing the business owner, the overall effect is not that dire in most cases.

An entrepreneur can operate one of two distinct business forms. The first type is the business the entrepreneur begins from scratch-- something that was an original idea or creation. In fact, this form of business is really at the heart of what it means to be an entrepreneur. The other type is to buy into a franchise (a business format or idea that was replicated and now exists in many other locations). In fact, the majority of businesses we all frequent these days are franchises.

With a franchise, you simply follow an already proven business plan. In other words, franchises are established businesses that started as an "original idea" at some point in the past. The original founders of the business achieve profit because the subsequent business owners (the "franchisees") pay an initial franchise fee (ranging from less than $10,000 to upwards of several hundred thousand dollars) as well as on-going royalties (a percentage of profits). In exchange for these payments, the franchisees receive initial training (many times at the franchise's base location) as well as promotional material, trade secrets, recipes (in the case of food franchises), and proprietary know-how. Franchises overall have a very healthy success rate, although this depends on many variables, such as the type of business, the work ethic of the franchisee, the employees the franchisee uses, and the willingness of the franchisee to adhere to the franchise system.

One can easily research franchises; in fact, annual rankings appear in several of the business magazines. However, just because a particular franchise has been successful over the years and boasts a high ranking in the popular literature doesn't necessarily mean it's the right one for you. It is a wise idea to choose a franchise that deals in something of interest to you and/or with which you have previous experience. This is not difficult, however. There is literally a franchise out there for every imaginable area of interest. Given the scope of available franchises (from every conceivable genre of fast food to mobile oil changing services to child education), it behooves one to give some thought to the question, "What do I want to be doing every day?".

Franchising certainly has a place in today's economy. The simple fact that the majority of businesses out there are franchises points to this fact. Overall, franchises possess a better success rate than "go it alone" type businesses. Although I have never owned a franchise, I feel this route will appeal to a certain segment of potential business owners, especially first-timers. In fact, a common thought among franchisees is they feel that while in business for themselves, they are operating within a larger structure. In other words, they retain a majority of the control over day-to-day operation but the corporate headquarters provides a great deal of support on the strategic level, not to mention national advertising campaigns intended for the benefit of all franchisees.

However, a successful franchise owner will be willing to give up a large amount of operational ("big-picture") control and succumb to the wishes of the corporate office when it comes to things like pricing, products, services offered, quality, hours of operation, etc. But again, there is a very real financial cost involved in return for the support, training and proprietary knowledge-- an initial franchise fee as well as a percentage of revenue (royalties) paid on a regular basis (usually monthly). Moreover, although buying into a franchise may be less risky than an original creation, the potential payoff may not be as great either, and many franchise owners end up operating several outlets in order to generate a sufficient income.

Which type of business is right for you? The final decision of whether to choose a franchise or to go your own way really depends on your personality (can you work within the franchise system? If not, they can potentially close you down), your prior business and entrepreneurial experience, and whether you already have a somewhat unique product/service/method of delivery that you could capitalize on. However, I would say if you really want to "call the shots," go the latter route. This way, you have total control over every aspect of your business, from the type of signs you choose to hang in your windows to the price you charge for the products or services you sell. Not to mention the fact that you avoid paying those annoying up-front and royalty fees. I have chosen this route with my various businesses. One additional thought-- the psychological satisfaction of running your own unique business is something you cannot put a price tag on.

In sum, there are millions of self-employed individuals who have been successful with either route. Therefore, the final decision really is dependent on your own personal circumstances. While full-time entrepreneurship may not be for everyone, I believe almost everyone in this country has some degree of entrepreneurial drive and can harness it if given the chance. In fact, many small business owners started with a part-time venture working out of their homes. This is another option for those who don't feel they can make the leap to full-time business operator overnight.

As for me, I have been an entrepreneur for over seven years as of this writing, first with real estate and then with my retail businesses along the beautiful San Antonio Riverwalk. I can say while it certainly has not been easy, it's been one of the most satisfying periods of my life. To be your own boss, to feel you truly hold your own destiny in your hands, is frightening in a sense but also extremely gratifying. I feel my own economic future is controlled by the person who cares about it most-- me! When I stop and ponder how much progress I've made over the years and how much I've learned and grown, without a corporate office to train me, support me and provide me with instructions, I get goosebumps. I am literally master of my destiny.

In the next chapter I want to give you more of a background as to what got me interested in being self-employed, what my experience with real estate was like, how I transitioned from real estate into retail and some fundamental principles of entrepreneurship I've learned along the way. I'd be the first one to admit I have a long way to go before I could consider myself in the same league as many other well-known business owners who we see in the media today. However, I am proud to have overcome all of the obstacles thrown in my way in order to arrive at the point where I am today.

Chapter II
Real Estate

Let me begin by giving you a little background as to how I arrived at this point. I actually started around the spring of 2004 as an entrepreneur, but in the field of real estate. I had been living in San Antonio, TX since the early 1990s, was on my way out from civil service and looking for something financially viable to pursue as well as something that would fit my unique circumstances. I obtained a copy of one of the more popular real estate courses on television at the time, and I was hooked immediately. I repeatedly listened to the CDs while I was driving or doing other activities and soon I felt I was ready to take the plunge.

While in San Antonio, I saw a small ad in the newspaper by a realtor who said he specialized in foreclosures, and decided to give him a call. We hit it off right away and soon thereafter, I was making offers on smaller-sized foreclosed homes. Foreclosures are somewhat different than normal "For Sale by Owner" (FSBO) type homes, as you essentially put in bids for the property in question up to a certain deadline, and one never knows what other investors are bidding. I had a friend, Henry, who was also interested in going in with me. Amazingly enough to us at the time, after putting in several offers, one of our foreclosure offers was accepted! We were extremely excited about it and began to go through the process of obtaining financing to close on it. Although it really wasn't that expensive, I had learned in the real estate course to never use your own money if possible; always use what they call OPM-- "other people's money." Although we had both purchased homes to live in, neither of us had ever bought an investment property. After a few weeks and relatively little incident, we were able to close on the house, and it officially was ours.

The house was about twenty years old, had three bedrooms and two baths, and was located in a residential area of San Antonio. The neighborhood was middle class and we thought the house would make a good rental unit, but it was in rather bad shape from a cosmetic point of view. It needed painting inside and out, new kitchen linoleum, new carpet, new fixtures, etc. Neither Henry nor I were very handy, so we had to hire different people to help us with different stages of the process. This was a challenge in and of itself, and frankly not something that I had given a lot of thought to beforehand. I guess I had a naive view of how contractors (and those who pose as contractors) operate. Nevertheless, after about two months, we were ready to rent out the property.

After placing an ad in the city newspaper, we began receiving calls from potential renters and eventually went with a family who received Section Eight (public housing) assistance. Although we were not familiar with Section Eight beforehand, after thinking about it Henry and I decided that it might very well work to our favor, as over half of the rent would be in the form of guaranteed income (from the county). After getting that property fixed up and rented out (with the bonus of having part of the rent as guaranteed income), we began the process of looking for more houses. Actually, I was the one who went out with the realtor on a day-to-day basis, as Henry was still working full-time. I submitted many offers, on FSBO homes as well as foreclosures, and several of them were accepted. By early fall of that year, we owned four single-family homes.

At this point we were getting really excited, and it started to feel that we were truly on our way to becoming real estate moguls. We continued our frantic pace of looking for properties, submitting offers, having some accepted, and then going through the closing process. Although now we had tenants to deal with, it was enjoyable and for the most part, the tenants seemed decent. Henry was the one who dealt with tenants most of the time, as he had grown up around that sort of thing (his parents had owned rental property since before he was born) and he enjoyed collecting the money and making sure all the new mortgages were paid. For a while, we were closing on about one property per month. We had four by August, six by October, and ten by January 2005! At that point, the administrative side of things was really becoming a time consuming process, but it was not overwhelming for Henry. Although I tried to help, I really didn't enjoy that end of things (dealing with tenants) and much preferred looking for new properties. Additionally, due to family issues, I was dividing my time between Florida and San Antonio during this time, so I left most of the day-to-day operations to Henry. I even gave him Power of Attorney in case I couldn't make it back to town for a closing that we might have.

In early 2005, with the real estate market still very strong all over the country, we decided to start going a much different direction-- that of acquiring more upscale homes. The single-family homes we had picked up all of the previous year had been relatively inexpensive, but we now were looking at properties with values several times higher. There were quite a few of these types of homes being built in San Antonio at this time, and some very nice gated communities were springing up in certain parts of the city. I had begun to meet some other real estate investors who were into these types of properties, and they convinced me that this was where the real money was to be made and not to waste my time with those inexpensive type houses that I had been picking up the previous year. We thus began to look in one of the more upscale new neighborhoods and quickly thereafter put in an offer on a FSBO property with an asking price higher than we had ever done before. However, we thought the offer seemed reasonable given the fact that it was in a beautiful gated community in one of the more exclusive areas of the city. In fact, it seemed like a great bargain.

All went according to plan, and we successfully closed on the property a few weeks later. We weren't sure if we wanted to rent the property to high-end tenants or live in it for a while and then resell it, but we decided on the latter. In other words, Henry moved in (I already had a home at that point) and paid the larger share of the mortgage. I visited him frequently there, and I must admit I enjoyed spending time at the property as well as in the gated community itself. It was a different world-- totally removed from the rest of the city. It almost seemed that we were in a posh part of Southern California.

As time went by, I continued to search for what I considered undervalued properties, but increasingly I did it without Henry. He was still working full-time and had his hands full with the smaller rental units, which by mid-2005 numbered in the range of twelve or thirteen. In other words, he was ready to enter the next phase of things, the "maintenance/holding" phase. However, I was addicted to the real estate game. I now had several realtors at my disposal, and continued to look for higher-end homes. I felt that there was nowhere to go but up for these homes and I couldn't go wrong since they were undervalued in terms of the sales price vs. the appraised value. By 2006, I individually owned four or five upscale homes. I had been successful in finding tenants to live in each of them and having the rental income be approximately equal to the mortgage payment on each (sometimes a bit more, sometimes a bit less). I felt that even if I weren't making any cash flow on any of them, I would be all right considering that I bought each for a good price and planned to be able to sell them at some point for a healthy profit.

By 2007, however, I began to feel the weight of large mortgage payments, dealing with my own tenants, and overseeing maintenance and repair issues. Although I felt that each of these would be good investments over the long-term, as the real estate market in San Antonio had not overheated like in much of the country, I decided to begin disposing of my properties. In addition to the upscale homes I owned in my own name (the other smaller investment properties were in both of our names), I had both a residence and commercial building in the Florida Panhandle, the latter of which I had rehabbed and had on the market for sale. Obviously, I had a full plate. I enlisted the assistance of different realtors (I have never been one to "put all my eggs in one basket") and got each property on the market. Although my cash reserves were dwindling, I still felt that each of these homes represented a good investment, as what I owed on them was less than the appraisal value. Eventually, one by one, I was able to dispose of these properties, including the one in Florida. By the time I took into account realtors' fees and other closing costs, the profit was decent but perhaps not the lavish windfall I had hoped for.

We also began selling off the smaller single-family homes around the middle part of 2007 as well. Part of the reason for this was that Henry felt he could not fully manage the properties since he had also begun a Ph.D. program a year or two earlier and had told me on more than one occasion that he never intended to be a long-term property owner. His idea was to use real estate as a financial "lever" to catapult us to the next level financially. We began looking for realtors who would be good candidates to help us list and sell these properties, and came across a couple who were willing to forego the usual three percent commission and do it for one percent if they could simply put their sign in the yard and get their name out in the public. I have found that there are so many realtors out there (the last time I heard, the city of San Antonio has approximately eight thousand active agents), that competition is fierce and that many are willing to list and promote a property for much less than the standard three percent sales commission. We successfully sold off three of our smaller homes in the latter part of 2007 and a couple more over each of the next few years. As it stands now, we only have three of the original single-family homes, (one of which Henry currently occupies, so essentially two rental units).

Tenants, of course, are a blessing and a curse. They are a blessing because they are paying the mortgage for you on a particular property and perhaps, if you're lucky, even providing you with a little cash flow. However, they are a curse in almost every other way. In general terms, with a few exceptions, I have found that many tenants really don't care much about your property and will tear up, destroy and expect you to fix things that many times they broke (either directly or indirectly through negligence and abuse). After dealing with tenants for over seven years now, I can say that I've seen some of the worst of human nature. Although many tenants are decent people, there is enough of the bad kind to give any potential property owner pause for reflection.

In my mind, tenants adhere to the "bell curve" phenomenon that accurately describes much of what happens in nature and society. If you are not aware of the bell curve, it states that most of whatever you happen to be measuring falls within the bulk of the curve, indicating that they are somewhat average or typical. One side of the curve holds a few samples that actually are above average or exceptional. On the other side of the curve, however, you have exactly the opposite-- samples that are below average. How does this apply then to tenants? From what I have observed, most tenants are about average. They don't do much to keep the property up, but don't actively destroy either. They normally pay the rent properly, but you might have to keep after them on occasion. I estimate this represents about eighty percent of the tenants that a property owner will encounter. Another ten percent will be above average, and will go out of their way to keep the property up, pay rent on or before the deadline, etc. In other words, they treat the property as if it's their own. The remaining ten percent, however, are below average. This type of tenant will tear up, destroy, and generally cause mayhem in the property. They will not pay rent properly and you will be forced to keep after them, threaten them with "Three Day Notices" (the first step toward eviction), and generally be a headache that you can't wait to see leave.

There is one family of tenants who comes to mind that should scare off any potential property investors/landlords who are "on the fence" about renting out property. Henry and I had a family in the first part of 2006 to move into a three bedroom, two bath home that was one of the first he and I acquired. It was a couple in their early 60s with a daughter in her early to mid-20s who had a small child of her own. They were very nice and appreciate that we were willing to let them rent the home. As tenants, in fact, they were decent for the majority of their time with us. However, they were frequently late with rent and toward the end had to start "breaking up" the rent; in other words, paying half at the beginning of the month and half a couple of weeks later. By the way, as a side note, I have found that when a tenant has to begin paying rent like this, it's usually a sign that the end is near.

Around June 2007, the wife called Henry and told him that they were having problems (they seemed to have an endless stream of problems-- with their children, health, Social Security payment, etc.) and they would not be able to pay rent until later in the month. We were almost at the end of our rope with them anyway and so Henry eventually gave them a "Three Day Notice to Pay or Quit," which as I mentioned, is essentially the first step toward eviction. In the rental business, you have to advise tenants in writing that they have three days to pay rent or else face the consequences, which means that you are legally able to file an eviction notice with the Justice of the Peace.

It was always hard dealing with them because the wife would always start crying on the phone with Henry. In our minds, it was a ploy to garner sympathy. He and I were both rather softhearted to be property owners; however, one toughens up quickly in the rental business. It got to the point (well beyond the initial three days) where Henry told them that he had no choice but to file an eviction notice. They apparently were not even home during this time due to their current family crisis, whatever that happened to be. Henry and I drove over to the property to look around and assess the situation.

When we arrived, we found the garage door about three quarters of the way closed, but from underneath we could tell that the garage was full of random clutter. When we opened the garage door, we discovered the entire garage full of junk and clutter-- clothes, old toys, old furniture, boxes, papers, old magazines, books, etc.-- literally from the floor to the ceiling. In fact, we had to clear a path to gain access to the garage door leading to the kitchen. Once inside, we were almost overcome with stench and the sight of rotting food, dog feces on the carpet, cat food on the floor, and general refuse and filth throughout the house. Because there was no furniture left, only refuse, the logical assumption was that the family had decided to abandon the property. This is actually somewhat common after a property owner issues (or threatens to issue) a Three Day Notice. Tenants will receive the note, and of course not wishing to go to court, packs up what they can, and leave "by the dark of night." After assessing the situation, we realized that we would need to start taking matters into our own hands. However, this was something we couldn't do alone.

We had been renting to a Hispanic family in one of our other properties since early 2005. They had always struggled with the rent, but one thing that they always were good for is helping us clean and fix up properties. The husband, Johnny, was very handy and his wife, Marta, was a very sturdy, strong woman who could work harder than most men I know. So we immediately called them to inform them of the situation and how we needed to get started cleaning up. Fortunately, they showed up a couple of hours later with cleaning supplies, buckets, and rubber gloves in hand.

Before going any further, Henry wisely decided to take dozens of pictures of the property to document the destruction they had left. A word to the wise for all potential property investors/landlords is to invest in a good digital camera. It is a smart idea always to take pictures of the property when tenants destroy and/or abandon your property. After taking pictures and getting in touch with

Johnny and Marta, Henry set out to work. His idea was to bag up all the tenants' garbage and refuse (he had bought a box of industrial strength trash bags solely for that purpose) and began bagging up and placing the bags out by the curb.

After a day of cleaning, he called the tenants and reprimanded them for the condition of the property, and told them that they needed to get their remaining junk or we would dispose of it. They were not happy about that (tenants never think that their mess is really that bad, and never admit guilt), but Henry stuck to his guns. After a couple of days of hard work, with Johnny and Marta's son helping as well, the garage was cleaned out and most of the refuse was out of the house. There had been dog feces on the carpet in the master bedroom, so they ended up ripping up the carpet and placing it out by the curb. Fortunately, Johnny had a truck, so they began hauling the garbage bags and the old carpet to the city dump. The ex-tenants came during the evening hours to pick up some of the bags of their items and may have tried to get into the house; but by that time, Henry had already changed the locks on the doors. Some of the neighbors who Henry talked to during those days indicated the husband seemed to suffer from a sort of "hoarding" compulsion and that he literally would bring home things he found in dumpsters. If you could have seen the garage, this supposition made complete sense. To top it all off, after a few days we discovered that there was a major flea problem in the house, so we had to fog the house several times in order to kill them all.

Our idea was to get the house ready to put on the market for sale. After we cleaned the house, we started on the rehab. We decided just to go for a cosmetic type fix-up, as the house essentially was in decent shape, and we didn't really want to put more than a nominal amount into it. We decided to have Johnny's family paint the entire interior, lay down linoleum tile, re-screen the back patio, as well as other cosmetic repairs. The three of them worked on it every day for three or four weeks, after which it looked quite attractive. I even had the garage door fixed (it apparently had not been working for several years, and having tenants that abused it didn't help). Henry and I then decided to put it on the market for sale. It was one of our first acquired properties and had been a foreclosure, so we owed less on it than what we otherwise would have. One of the things that Henry had also been working on was getting his realtor's license, which would help us to buy and sell property less expensively. In case you're not aware, when you buy a house, you don't pay any realtors' fees. However, when you sell a house, you normally pay six percent of the sales price of the property-- three percent for your realtor and three percent for the buyer's realtor. If we could list it ourselves, we could potentially save several thousand dollars per transaction.

After we listed it on the market for sale, Henry decided to move into the property to "house sit" until the property sold. There is a debate in the real estate world about the better way to leave a house when it is on the market-totally empty or furnished. If it is empty, the potential buyers get an idea of the intricacies of the property layout and can imagine how they would furnish the property. If there is furniture in the property (the "lived in" look), it may feel a bit more inviting to the potential buyers and might hide any of the home imperfections a bit better. Generally, the consensus is that unless you have very nice furnishings, leave the home empty for buyers. However, in this case, I think Henry wanted to house sit for a couple of reasons. First, he could continue to work on little things around the house (there are always things to fix in an older home) and keep the lawn manicured a little easier. Second, we had always liked this home and felt that it would be nice to have the chance to live in it before we sold it. We listed it for "fair market value" for the area-- a very established, family-oriented neighborhood with many amenities (the HOA pool was almost Olympic size) and schools nearby. Therefore, it was definitely a desirable area for families looking in that price range.

We had a couple of showings on the house during the latter part of that summer, and after about six weeks we got an offer for very close to what our asking price was. It turned out to be a father buying the property for his son to live in while he attended college in San Antonio (they were coming from an area of Southeast Texas called the Rio Grande Valley). Fortunately, the home inspector just had a few things that he wanted us to do in order to go forward. In October, we closed the deal; Henry quickly got his belongings out, and we were able to sell the property for a rather healthy profit (although a great deal of headache). If I could point to a property of ours that was really the textbook example of buying a foreclosure, renting it out for a few years, and then fixing up and selling for a decent profit, it would be this one.

Not long after selling this house, another incident occurred-- a fire in a property we owned in the same subdivision. A property owner pays dwelling insurance on an annual basis and never really expects to have to use it. However, on this particular occasion, we were very grateful that we had it. One morning Henry got up to find several messages in his cell phone voice mail. After listening to each of them several times, he understood what had happened-- there had been a fire the previous night in one of our properties. The woman renting it was in her mid-50s, who never seemed to be "all there" mentally. We rented to her originally about six months prior because her adult son came with her to look at the property, and we were under the impression (or they led us to believe) that the two of them would be living in the home. The home, although 25 years old, was very nice and spacious, as it was two stories with four bedrooms, an enclosed garage, and a back room added on.

We rushed over to the property as soon as we could and got the whole story from the fire department. According to what the tenant stated, she put some ice cream in the microwave to defrost it, went upstairs, and when she came down a few minutes later saw flames shooting from out the top of the microwave, which ended up setting the kitchen on fire. Although the fire department put out the fire relatively quickly, there was smoke damage throughout the home, even upstairs. If you've never smelled the inside of a home after a fire has been through it, it's really a disgusting, almost nauseating, smell. Henry and I drove back over to the property that night after all the dust had settled (both literally and figuratively) and he went inside the house to look around and wanted me to come in, but I literally couldn't bear the stench.

The insurance company had immediately dispatched one of the flood and fire repair companies in town to start gutting the home and begin repairs, and we met with them several times over the course of the next couple of days as well as with the insurance adjustor. It was clear that it was an accident, and the insurance company seemed very cooperative and led us through the claims process. The police and fire department told her that she could not stay in the home anymore due to safety concerns, so we never really interacted with her after that point except over the phone a couple of times. It was all quite traumatic for all involved.

The repair company had begun removing all of the charred wood and other fire damaged parts of the home and placed a big industrial-sized dumpster in front of the house to put everything in. They were very efficient and were willing to charge the insurance company directly. After several months of rehab, we got the house back in shape. Actually, it was in better shape than before because now most all the interior and a good part of the exterior were new. The insurance claim check was for almost exactly what the repair bill was. Coincidence? Makes you wonder.

We put it on the market and amazingly, we were able to sell it. Actually, we sold it to an investor acquaintance of ours who had plans to rent it out for around $1500 a month (the most I had been able to get was about $1250). We gave it to him for a good price since no outside realtors were involved, and as a result, we were down one more property.

Around June 2009, something else happened at one of our properties that forced Henry to take matters into his own hands once more. A family who lived in our only two bedroom home was several weeks late on the rent. Again, Henry and I have always attempted to play by the rules, issuing a written Three Day Notice, then filing for formal eviction with the Justice of the Peace. As in many states, the laws in Texas are very much in favor of the tenants. Henry issued the Three Day Notice and then went back several days later to attempt to make contact with them in order to try to decide whether it was worth it to file a formal notice of eviction. We have found that many times just the threat of eviction is enough to convince people to pay up. He found that the door was unlocked, and decided to poke his head in to see what the condition of the house was. To his surprise and utter dismay, it seemed that the tenants had "half" moved out. In other words, the electricity was off and major pieces of furniture were gone; but there was trash, clothing, papers, dirty diapers, etc. strewn all over the floor. In the kitchen, they had left behind food in the refrigerator, which was now rotting and emitting a horrible stench due to the heat inside the house. There was even a dirty pot with leftover chili on the stove. Henry told me it was enough to make him want to vomit.

Henry and I immediately decided that he would not let this go on. It always upset us how people can be so destructive and care so little about something that is not their own. It's really amazing how tenants can live the way they do. Even though Henry and I have been tenants at different points in our lives, the difference is that we always respected the property that we happened to be living in at the time.

He immediately went to buy some industrial strength garbage bags and rubber gloves, came back to the property and started bagging up everything he could find-- clothes, dirty dishes in the sink, plastic toys on the floor, old bills, magazines, etc. In case you're not aware, the summers in San Antonio are extremely intense. Imagine the type of stench created in a house that had had no electricity (and thus no air conditioning) for several days or weeks, rotting food in the refrigerator, dirty dishes, pots and pans in the sink, and smelly clothes all over. Now imagine having to clean up a mess like this that you didn't create. Such are the joys of owning rental property.

Henry worked continuously for the whole day, bagging up trash and laying the bags out on the front sidewalk. As they had no trash pick-up service, Henry had no choice but to load up those bags and take them back to his house for pick-up there. At that moment, he later told me, he decided not to rent that house out again. He said he would rather fix it up and live there himself-- and that's exactly what he did. During the rest of the summer, he and Johnny painted the entire interior and replaced the kitchen faucet, window blinds, both toilets, and carpet throughout the house. As most of it was "sweat equity," he was able to do all of this for about $1500 (the carpet and padding itself was about $800 of that). Believe me, after that. it seemed like a brand new house. To top it off, he bought a little portable A/C unit for one of the windows to help cool down the house during the hot months.

After about six weeks of fix up, the house looked brand new on the inside and was livable and quite cozy. To top it off, last summer he pressure-washed the entire house, driveway, and front sidewalk and then repainted the entire exterior. He also replaced the bathroom faucets to a very elegant antique-type brass faucet. Now with a total makeover, the home is one that we should have for a long time.

By the end of 2009, we had successfully sold off around six properties. We now held around five rental units, which felt a little more sustainable. Henry would laugh about it when he thought about how crazy things got there for a while with twelve houses. He would say things like, "I woke up one morning and had twelve houses. It was like a bad dream." Of course, he was only half joking. That is to say, the rental business can be profitable, but it can be brutal and bring a grown man to tears at times (although Henry always handled it very well). Again, during a good part of this time he was working full-time and later a full-time graduate student, so he really had to juggle his time. With three properties (as it currently stands), it is even more manageable, and it feels like something that we can sustain and hopefully hold onto for the long-term. The ones that we still have are a couple of the ones that we picked up first (including our very first two, which we acquired during the summer of 2004) and another toward which we have always had a fondness toward. It's funny because you really can develop a connection with a house, even if you never live in it. Henry and I have had the opportunity to live in several of our properties over the years, and that helps even more to develop that connection.

There is one other point that I would like to make to any potential property investors/landlords. In a vast majority of the cases, it takes a great deal of time to build up any equity in the particular property. Equity is what the home is currently valued for minus its outstanding balance. For example, if you have a home that currently appraises for $100,000 and you owe $85,000 on it, your equity is $15,000. However, it generally takes years to build up any significant equity in a property. What's more, in order to actually make a profit on the eventual sale of the property, you must have enough equity to compensate for the literally thousands of dollars of closing costs (realtors' fees, title company fees, etc.). Going back to the previous example, if you estimate you have $15,000 in equity, you really have only about half that amount, maybe $7500. This is because when you sell a property, the aforementioned fees will absorb much of that "paper equity." Although it varies widely, the general rule of thumb is that you must hold onto a property for at least seven or eight years before you can build up enough equity to make a profit when you sell it. So then the question you must ask yourself is, "Can I deal with tenants for seven years or more just to make a little money?" Although this may come across as facetious, it is a very serious question that one must answer carefully and honestly.

In the spring of 2009, I began delving into a new sort of rental business, called the "luxury rental" market. In the spring of 2008, I purchased a very beautiful, 5500 square foot, Mediterranean-style home just north of San Antonio, at the base of the Texas Hill Country. Although I enjoyed living there immensely, as you can no doubt imagine the mortgage payment and upkeep on the property was a real budget-buster. In early 2009, I met a young woman who turned me on to something that I had never considered before-- the short-term rental market. This is actually a relatively new concept, and one which neither Henry nor I were familiar with, but were quickly attracted to.

The concept in itself is quite simple. You rent out a property for the short-term (anywhere from three nights to a week) to a family (or several families) and charge a premium for that stay. The rates for a high-end property can range anywhere from $300 to upwards of $500 or more per night. However, this also represents a bargain for the guests because on a per-person basis this normally comes out to be significantly less than what a hotel would charge on a nightly basis. Add to this the fact that the family can effectively enjoy all the luxuries of home (or more if it they were to rent a higher-end property) and be able to visit much more freely than in a hotel, cook, or watch movies together on the big-screen TV. My mind was doing summersaults imagining how much money I could potentially make with this venture. The only real downside was the number of people that might be in the house at any given time. Although we placed a capacity limit of ten persons, even this number places a strain on plumbing systems (as I would come to find out in spades during the first summer) and general wear and tear. Not to mention the fact that many people will surreptitiously attempt to bring in more than the permitted number of guests. Therefore, I suppose there is a downside, just as with everything else in life.

The young woman who initially told me about the opportunity also helped me place the house on one of several highly trafficked websites dedicated to the vacation rental business as well as develop a stand-alone website exclusively for my property. It was relatively simple to do, and Henry and I were both impressed with how many properties were available for short-term rental. In fact, there are hundreds just in the state of Texas, with literally thousands listed all across the U.S. and even internationally. Actually, Henry remembered that he and his extended family had stayed in a beachfront home that they rented short-term when his brother got married. Thus, we did have a bit of a precedent for doing this.

We designed a rental application form and obtained a fax number that would have faxes sent straight to my email. I already had the ability to accept credit cards since I had credit card merchant accounts at my retail stores. I just had the companies open a dedicated account for my new luxury rental business. Soon after we had the property posted on the website, I began receiving applications. In fact, the applications literally began to pour in. I would say that I received six or seven within the first two weeks of posting the property. Usually the actual reservations would be for a time slot six months or so in advance, as the future guests would be planning corporate getaways, family reunions, or summer vacations coming from the other side of the country.

Although the idea of luxury/vacation rental was relatively simple, the actual implementation from a logistical standpoint was rather difficult. Per the web designer's advice, I asked for a deposit of $500 via credit card when the future guest submitted the application. This amount was to dissuade anyone from making a frivolous reservation as well as to have some sort of indemnity against damage to the property. I experimented with deducting the deposit amount from the balance due (in other words, if the total bill were $3500, then they would simply owe $3000 after the deposit). In that sense, there really was no indemnity for any damage to the property. I also used the deposit in the traditional indemnity sense and refunded $500 (less any damages) to them approximately a week after they left. Both methods had their advantages and disadvantages, and I never really reached a conclusion as to which method was best. The former was much simpler to maneuver, while the latter protected me more.

As might be expected, the guests that stay in a luxury rental and pay "top dollar" are for the most part quite demanding. They usually expect everything to be just perfect-- from the arrangement of the furniture to how many towels are in each of the bathrooms. Initially I hired two sisters who lived in the area and who had many years of cleaning experience. One of the problems was that the house was simply so large-- there are five bedrooms, four bathrooms, a movie room and a playroom, not to mention two patios. That would be a lot for anyone to do, and generally I had to push them very hard to give the home what I called a "deep cleaning" (scrubbing of sinks and bathtubs, waxing of floors, oiling of cabinets, etc.) and not just a superficial cleaning (a simple vacuuming and light dusting). Although I paid them well (around $250 per cleaning), they always seemed to be dissatisfied with the way I treated them. My theory is that they resented working for and being "bossed around" by an Asian immigrant who seemed to be much more successful in life. Therefore, there was always friction there. They suddenly quit one day right before some guests were due to arrive. When the two sisters didn't show up, I was forced to clean the house myself before the guests got in. It was only later through hearsay that I discovered that they didn't care much for me. I went through several other helpers but never really found anyone with whom I was completely satisfied.

Another big logistical/planning issue was keeping track of when people were arriving and departing. Like I mentioned, during the first week or two of advertising, I received seven or eight applications, and by the end of May, I literally had the whole summer booked, sometimes with one group checking out in the morning and another arriving that afternoon. Obviously, this required tremendous planning not only in getting the home ready for the next party, but also in the accepting of applications. In other words, not to "double book" guests (have any overlap in the dates) was a constant concern. On the website, a calendar showed which dates were available at any given time. I took great care not to double book guests, and I believe this may have happened only once or twice (which is enough!). However, on the days that I had "back to back" guests, I was really under incredible pressure to get the house cleaned and ready for the next group to arrive. During my second summer of luxury rental, I tried not to book guests like this, but sometimes it's unavoidable-- guests want to come when they want to come. So on these types of days, I had to get whoever was helping me in the house and on-task quickly.

Once I realized how much money I could make with this business, I was hooked. However, there was just one small problem-- where would my family and I live during the days when guests were there? After considering the possibilities, I decided to rent an apartment in a new complex more toward town. Although this was somewhat of a sacrifice, both financially and psychologically, it seemed to work out relatively well. During the summer months, I had the property rented out approximately five nights a week (most groups stayed at least three or four nights, with two nights being my minimum). So on those nights we obviously would have to go to the apartment. However, the house was vacant enough of the time that we could come back occasionally and experience the "ahhhh!" feeling as if returning home after a trip of some sort. During the non-peak months, we only had maybe two guests a month, so it wasn't that big of an issue during that time. In fact, one of the great things about the luxury rental website was I could block dates that I wanted to reserve for myself, such as around Thanksgiving and Christmas. Anyone looking for those dates would just see that these were not available, not necessarily that I was actually staying there. Thus, I retained complete control over when I wanted to rent the property out.

Although the operation was very profitable, it was not without headache. One of the primary problems was with the Home Owners' Association. As you can imagine, they did not care for the idea of renting the property out like this. I did a good job of staying off their radar, although I didn't realize I was doing anything wrong at the time by renting out the home. However, several incidents with neighbors called it to their attention. One of the most memorable was an incident that occurred with the septic tank (as we are well outside the city limits, there is no city sewer system). As I alluded to previously, one of the challenges I faced when renting to a group was ensuring that there were no more than ten people in the home. I felt that any more than that would place undue stress on the plumbing system and other aspects of wear and tear. However, making sure about the number was not an easy task. One group, claiming nine or ten guests, actually had something in the order of eighteen or nineteen. In other words, people sleeping on the floor, on the couches, etc. This was undoubtedly overwhelming for the home's plumbing system, despite the size of the home and number of bathrooms.

After a day or two, the septic tank began to beep loudly, indicating that it needed servicing. It then began to overflow with human waste into the neighbor's yard! Once I realized the situation, I immediately called a septic tank service. The technician told me that the tank began acting like that because it was completely overwhelmed and full, no doubt in large part to nearly twenty people using the toilets over a period of several days. Fortunately, the group only stayed about three nights. Obviously, I kept their deposit, although they had the nerve to get angry with me for keeping it. However, I did get a nasty letter from the HOA. Although I felt I needed to honor the reservations that were scheduled for the rest of the summer, I didn't make any new ones for the rest of the year and was very careful regarding quality control with the remainder of the guests that I had.

The second year, things seemed to go a little smoother, as I now had one year of the luxury rental business under my belt and felt that over the winter I had been able to analyze my previous missteps and learn from them. Like I mentioned previously, I no longer used the "two sisters"-- apparently they got upset with me because they felt like I was taking advantage of them (paying them *only* $250 for a cleaning). Fortunately, I was able to find someone else to help me who seemed to work well. However, it was just one person who was quite a bit slower and I felt I had to supervise her a good deal more. On the other hand, though, she had a good attitude and helped me with other things that I needed, like picking up little things for the house at the supermarket on days we were expecting guests. In addition, I learned to block a date on the calendar between guests, a sort of "buffer day." This was to avoid the stress of having back-to-back guests (a departure and an arrival on the same day). I felt like it didn't take away from the revenue at all, and it really lowered my stress level. I didn't feel that I was "under the gun" nearly as much (there was always the chance that my cleaning help would "flake out" on me during these times, which would put me in a severe bind).

All in all, I would say that for those property owners who fit certain criteria (have a nicer property that they wish to rent out, have readily available help, are not afraid to advertise on the internet, and are willing to be very "hands on"), luxury rental can be an extremely lucrative business. Again, from the rates that I've seen over the last few years, even a mid-level property can command anywhere from $100 to $250 a night, with the upper-end properties able to command upwards of $400 a night. However, like any business, it will require some planning, foresight, and the right mindset. If this sort of business appeals to you, I encourage you to do some research on the internet to find out more about it. Additionally, I would recommend going with one of several leading websites that have the majority of the listings and thus the customer traffic.

As I wind up this section on real estate, I would like to leave you with some final thoughts. Some hard-core investors will tell you that you should never develop any emotion whatsoever with your properties, but it's hard not to-- and who's to say that it's really a bad thing? I mean, an investment property is different from a paper investment, like a stock or a mutual fund. I've owned mutual funds that I've sold or readjusted because they had been underperforming or no longer fit my needs and then not given it a second thought. However, a property is something that you can walk around in, live in, make memories in, etc. and can be very profitable (although it's a tremendous amount of work and responsibility). If you feel a connection with a property, you may be more motivated to take care of it, encourage your tenants to take care of it, and hold onto it over the long-term. However, of course you should use your common sense and follow the old adage of, "Everything in moderation." You don't want to go overboard on fixing up the property between tenants or buying expensive appliances for them, because most likely they will not take the best care of them. However, you do want to find that balance between maintaining the property adequately and your going broke to make it feel more luxurious than it needs to be. Just remember that a good coat of paint and a good professional carpet cleaning will go a long way toward making the property livable and keeping the tenants happy without you going broke in the process.

Chapter III

Real Estate Tips

Real estate can be very profitable, but it's not nearly as easy as those late-night real estate course infomercials would have you to believe. I want to leave you with something tangible from my years in the real estate business, and thus present you with some ideas that I have distilled regarding what to do (and not to do) based on my experiences. Thus, the following are my "Top Ten Tips for Investing in Real Estate."

1. *Add properties slowly.* This is one mistake I believe Henry and I made that likely hurt us in the long run. During our acquisition phase from mid-2004 to the spring of 2005, we closed on twelve properties-- that's more than one per month. It was a heady feeling, to say the least, picking up properties at this rate and seeing your net worth, at least on paper, skyrocket. Henry, who has made a habit of calculating his net worth at the end of each year, said he saw his net worth rise over $100,000 due to the combined equity that we calculated we had in the properties. However, there were a couple of things wrong with this approach. Although on paper this may have been true, the equity in the properties was far from a sure thing. That is to say, we would have had to *sell* the individual properties before we realized any of this equity. These calculations can look great on paper, but the

real estate market is relatively illiquid (hard to convert to cash). Thus, you calculate your equity based on the recent comparable sales of similar properties in that area. However, when it comes time to sell your respective property, countless things can affect whether you are successful in selling the property for the price you had envisioned at the outset. Although San Antonio is known for having a relatively stable real estate market, putting a property on the market and selling it for the desired price involves many factors and a good deal of luck.

Something else that I believe compromised our endeavor was the fact that neither of us had managed property before. Such factors as dealing with tenants, collecting rent, maintaining properties, etc. were things we had never before encountered. Although Henry's parents had owned rental property in his hometown since before he was born, he had never taken an interest in it growing up. So imagine going from zero experience dealing with this type of thing to owning twelve properties in less than a year. In other words, there was a huge learning curve. Henry and I learned very quickly (although we did make many mistakes along the way), but at the end we found that it was simply too much. I was always more interested in going out to look for even *more* property to buy and not as interested in actually maintaining the ones we already *owned*.

Looking back on it, I regret not helping more in the day-to-day upkeep of the properties and dealing with tenants. To his credit, Henry handled it extremely well. I believe that we could have held onto more of the properties for a longer period than we actually did if we had added properties *slowly* and therefore had a more manageable learning curve. In retrospect, I accept full responsibility for this mistake, as I was the one pushing us to pick up more and more properties.

2. *Learn all you can from books and courses, but be ready to make changes and adapt.* When Henry and I first delved into real estate, I listened to one of the popular real estate courses repeatedly in my car as I drove around town. It was one of the courses advertised on late-night TV during this time; it came with a book and a set of CDs. The way we got into real estate in the first place was through a business class that Henry had been teaching at one of the local universities. A course requirement that Henry always asked of his students was a final project. One of the students did hers on real estate, and brought the course into class to show everyone. Henry expressed interest, and she literally gave it to him (she said she had ordered it the previous year and never done anything with it). He listened to it, passed it along to me and the rest is history.

After listening to the CDs repeatedly for a period of several months (and continuing even as we began to acquire properties), I felt like I had a solid foundation in the basics of property investment. As this was the early to mid-2000s, loans were easy to come by. The banks were lending very easily and readily, unlike the current loan conditions as of 2011 with the housing market crash. Hence, we were able to acquire properties extremely rapidly. Although the book knowledge that I picked up in general, and through this course in particular, served us well, we definitely faced a steep learning curve as we progressed through the acquisition phase and then into the maintenance phase of things.

We always looked back to the things that we had read and listened to, and kept up with the current literature in the popular personal finance magazines on the subject, but we always tried to remember that the reality could be (and often was) quite a bit different. That is to say, we had to maintain an open mind and remember that the basic principles of real estate investing had to be modifiable according to our specific local market and our particular circumstances. Overall, we did a formidable job in this regard. I have several acquaintances who also studied similar real estate courses but did not have the same level of achievement later. Although I can't be sure, I suspect that one reason for this was their inability to make the translation from the book/audio knowledge to the application of that knowledge and the flexible approach that many times this entails. I would encourage you to learn all you can about real estate or whatever field you're interested in, but also to maintain a flexible mindset. Realize that regardless of how much you think you know, there will always be challenges to overcome.

3. *Pay your mortgages promptly and don't let yourself get behind.* This habit will serve you well throughout your property-investing career. It's very easy to collect the rental revenue for the month and then not pay all of your mortgage payments-- in other words, to do something else with that money (many times on things that have nothing to do with the properties). However, doing this will bring you nothing but heartache and frustration in your quest to keep the properties over the medium- to long-term. Sure, you can always play catch-up with your mortgage payments, but it's not a good idea. First, the mortgage company is going to charge you late fees. These can be anywhere from $20 to $40 per month depending on the mortgage servicer and amount of the mortgage. Second, if you are more than thirty days late on the mortgage, they report it to the credit bureaus, which will leave a negative mark that will last for up to seven years. It's amazing, but I've come to learn that even one late payment on something like this can have a very big (and in my view a disproportionate) impact on your credit score, knocking it down anywhere from 20 to 50 points. Even though you think your credit score has no bearing on your daily life, it in fact does. It can affect the ease with which you acquire future properties, your interest rate, your ability to acquire new credit cards, and your ability to get a car loan or any other type of consumer credit. Even if you currently have a credit card, the company can raise your rate due to the increased risk perception.

Third, it's very difficult to make up these missed payments, even if they don't seem that big. Think about the following scenario-- let's imagine your monthly payment on a property is $600. Your car breaks down one month, and you feel that you have to use the rent money from the property to fix your car. Now, the following month, you have to pay not only the $600 for the current month, but the $600 payment from the previous month for a total of $1200 (plus late fees). Where would you get the money to pay this amount if you already are struggling to pay one month's mortgage payment? Do yourself a favor and keep up with your mortgage payments. You should have a "rainy day" fund for your unexpected personal expenses and let rental revenue go exclusively toward making mortgage payments.

4. *If you have a problem, be sure to let your mortgage company know.* This harkens back to the previous lesson. If you do happen to get in a bind for whatever reason, be sure to communicate your problem to the mortgage company. Many people (myself included) shy away from calling and speaking with their mortgage company, because to be honest, it is a rather unpleasant experience. They always read off several legal disclaimers informing you that they are debt collectors and that any information you provide may be used for that purpose. Who wants to speak with someone like that? However, it is imperative that you begin speaking with them soon- maybe not if you're only going to be a couple of weeks (or maybe a month) late, because they will report you

as late to the credit bureaus regardless of whether or not you communicate with them. However, once you pass around the two-month point of being delinquent, you definitely want to be in contact. You have to be more than 90 days late to be susceptible to foreclosure proceedings. Although pre-foreclosure would not necessarily begin on the 91st day, you are exposing yourself to the possibility after this point. Therefore, if you are a month late but catch up quickly, there may be no reason to speak with customer service at the mortgage servicer. However, the bottom line is that they want you to be able to make your monthly payment because that is also in their best interest.

In this era of modern finance, in most cases the mortgage servicer (the people you send your monthly check to) does not ultimately own (or "hold") your mortgage. Frequently, once the mortgage is "originated," the servicer sells the mortgage to an investment bank of some sort. The bank then packages it with other similar mortgages, and then sells them to investors as bonds called Collateralized Debt Obligations. Pension funds, retirement funds, and other investment vehicles then hold these bonds. In other words, your mortgage is a financial obligation that is being bought and sold on the open market. The company that appears to be the holder of your mortgage is actually just collecting the money every month. The company has long since "sold off" your mortgage, received money for it, and now plays just a relatively small role in the life of your mortgage.

This is one of the reasons for the most recent financial crisis. Lenders made many loans that they shouldn't have because they knew that very soon after they made the mortgage loans, they would divest themselves of them. So, in truth, they faced minimal risk if the homeowner defaulted on the mortgage. The ultimate bearer of risk would be the investor who bought the bond, which was comprised of not only a minute portion of your mortgage, but also small portions of thousands of other similar mortgages. Many times the lenders were rewarded for making the riskiest of loans because the interest rate to the borrower (and ultimately the payment to the bondholder) would be higher. These loans could also perhaps involve other predatory lending practices, such as "interest only" loans in which the mortgage principal (the amount you actually borrow for the home) was literally *never reduced*-- the borrower paid only the mortgage *interest* every month. In my mind, this is evil in its purest form.

In sum, don't view the mortgage company (or "servicer" as they are many times referred to) as your friend. They are a debt collector, and they will report you as delinquent if you are more than thirty days late and will pester you with letters and phone calls, especially past the sixty-day point. However, unless you plan to pay off your property, they are unavoidable and an entity that you must live with. Your best course of action is to pay your mortgage(s) promptly before the fifteenth of the month in order to avoid any sort of possible late fees.

5. *Go through your monthly statements with a "fine tooth comb."* Your mortgage statements are your primary source of monthly information regarding your property. It is normally a very detailed statement which among other things, provides you with the principal balance, current interest rate, and escrow balance, which is the amount that you have on reserve with them to cover property taxes and insurance. We have always kept a file on each of our properties, and this is something that I always keep for the duration of our ownership of the property.

Besides this primary information, the mortgage statement will also indicate when your last payment was received, how much went to principal vs. interest vs. escrow, and if there were any late charges assessed. Although most of the time all of this information is correct, you always want to make it a point to sit down and go through these to check for any errors, changes in interest rates (if you have an adjustable rate mortgage) or escrow amounts. Even if your interest rate is fixed, the amount that is siphoned off to escrow can vary from year to year depending on the mortgage company's projections of the upcoming year's property taxes and dwelling insurance rates. Also, be on the lookout for any additional miscellaneous fees that the servicer may have assessed, especially if you are unfortunate enough to get slightly behind in your payments.

If you remit payment after the fifteenth of each month, normally the mortgage companies will begin to charge rather nominal late fees, but if you reach beyond the 60 or 90-day point, there will be fees galore related to "pre-foreclosure" type activities. Pre-foreclosure is a period in which they are preparing potentially to take your property into foreclosure (which is an extremely long process) but during which you can still bring the loan current. From my experience, this is usually in the 90 to 120-day past due range. Anything up to 90 days is usually safe from any danger of foreclosure, but they will begin to charge you all sorts of miscellaneous fees, which will appear on your monthly statement. However, after 120 days, you are in prime foreclosure territory, and it will usually take dealing with the "loss mitigation" department to save the property.

The bottom line is that mortgage companies make mistakes, just like any other business. They are usually dealing with hundreds of thousands to literally millions of mortgages (in the case of the large national banks), so mistakes can happen, even though they are relatively rare. However, even if there are no mistakes, it is in your best interest to keep up with the monthly statements in order to track outstanding balances, escrow amounts, amount going to principal (which should increase over the years of ownership), and other key pieces of information related to your properties. Additionally, the more properties you own, the more vital it is to keep up with these statements and file them in your respective property folders for future reference.

6. *It is okay to be friendly with tenants, but do not let them mistake that for weakness.* Tenants are one of the fundamental aspects of your investment property business. The rental revenue that they pay you every month is the lifeblood of your business-- without it, you would most likely lose your properties within a matter of a few short months. Besides that, they are actually living in a home that you own, pay property taxes and insurance on, and maintain with repairs. There is, therefore, a natural tendency for you as the property owner to feel a sort of empathy towards them, especially if you are by nature a friendly and people-oriented person. I have felt this way towards tenants, especially those who have been with us for long periods of time, take exceptionally good care of the property, or always pay rent in a timely manner. Some of these tenants have been so good that I have wanted to give them Christmas gifts, such as a fruit basket or turkey. However, I am glad I didn't, because I have learned we must maintain a boundary with tenants.

Many tenants are wonderful people, but there is a power distance between you as the property owner and them as the tenants. If you begin to treat them too much like friends or family, a great temptation begins to creep in for them to begin to ask for favors. These can be things such as paying rent late, paying the rent in parts (half at the beginning of the month and half mid-month, etc.), or other things that begin to test your relationship and put you in somewhat of an awkward position. Therefore, I have found the best policy to follow is to maintain a friendly but slightly detached relationship with tenants for long-term success. In other words, pleasant but authoritative is advisable.

Have you ever had a boss (or been a boss) who tried to be friends with all the employees? If you were the employee in that situation, how did it make you feel? Most likely, at first you may have thought it was fun to have such a "cool" boss. However, after some time passed you probably felt that you didn't respect that person quite as much versus if he/she had simply tried to be pleasant, but somewhat detached and authoritative. You could say the same for the tenant-landlord relationship. The dynamic is very delicate. If you are the property owner, you want the tenant to respect you enough to pay you the rent properly, without excuses, and take care of the property. You don't want them to think that you will "understand" if they are a week late with the rent or that you will "work with them" regarding dividing the rent into two parts over the course of the month. Remember that the rental business is a business like any other and that while you respect the tenants as your "customers," you do expect them to live up to their end of the contract (paying rent on time, etc.) just as they expect you to live up to yours.

7. *Learn to do a few simple repairs yourself.* A corollary to this is to also learn enough about the more complex repairs (like with A/C units and plumbing) to know if someone is

trying to grossly overcharge. Yet another idea is to find some good handymen or repair companies you trust to help you with the inevitable things that will occur.

With this said, it is vital for you or your partner to learn how to do a few simple repairs yourselves. The first "landlord" repair that Henry and I learned to do was to change out the door locks on the houses after a tenant moved out (or when we purchased a house, took possession, and went inside for the first time). Actually, one of the handymen that helped us with our first property during the summer of 2004 showed Henry how to do it, and this knowledge has served us well over the course of the last seven years. I can't tell you how many times he has changed locks on houses since we have made it a habit of always changing locks after a tenant moves out. You can buy a new lock set at any hardware store for around $20 (or a multi-pack for about $35) and it comes with all of the necessary hardware and inner workings. What's more, once you have an "inventory" of locks, you can just switch them around among houses after someone moves out, so you don't have to buy new ones all the time. This little piece of knowledge has saved us hundreds of dollars over the years, not to mention provided us with a sense of confidence that we can deal with the challenges that arise with owning investment property. Since that time, Henry has also learned some basic plumbing, like changing out the water line tubing on toilets, replacing sink faucets, etc.

However, regardless of how much you think you have learned in this area, there are other repairs that only experts should do. A prime example of this is heating and air conditioning (commonly referred to as HVAC) work. These units are extremely advanced and very technical. In fact, the people who work in this field have to go to school, pass a final exam, and receive a license from the state that allows them to work in this field. The systems are simply too complex for the layperson to attempt, although there are simple things that we can all do to help maintain the systems, such as regularly changing the air filters. Nevertheless, even though we can't work on those systems, it is wise for us to gain a basic understanding of them so we will know when a technician or HVAC company is trying to cheat us. As with anything, after a while you begin to develop a sense of fair and proper pricing. Thus, I would encourage you to learn all you can about air conditioning systems, plumbing, etc. even if you don't think that you would ever be doing any of this kind of work yourself.

The other aspect of this, which I alluded to earlier, is to find a good repairperson. Fortunately, we have had some good handymen over the years. Johnny and his family were probably the ones who helped us the most, and since they also rented from us, Henry and I felt in a sense that we were "keeping it in the family." We would many times, especially for bigger jobs, pay him with a combination of cash and "rent credit" (in other words, deducting the labor from what he owed us for the rent), which seemed to work very well since most months he struggled to come up with rent money. Johnny was very good at fixing things and most of the time was very conscientious in the way that he went about doing his work. He and his family on more than one occasion totally revamped a home, and practically "brought back to life" several properties for me.

8. *Keep good records.* The act of keeping good records is a fundamental part of any investment strategy and/or business endeavor (we've always considered owning rental property to be a sort of hybrid between an investment and a business). However, it is *essential* to being a successful property investor. I would recommend keeping a file on each property you own, and being vigilant about filing documents, receipts, etc. into the respective property's file as soon as you get them.

Your paperwork history on a particular property begins really when a submitted property offer is accepted. You will most likely want to keep this as a sort of "foundation" upon which everything else is built. Of course, it will have the full property address, the buyers (you and any partners), the sellers, the price that you settled on, and other pertinent information (such as the realtors involved). Before closing, you will most likely have expenses, such as earnest money (a type of deposit, usually around $1000, that lets the sellers know that you are serious buyers), a property inspection, and other things related to your due diligence on the property. At closing (usually performed at a title company or a law office that deals in real estate), you will remit any additional money due and sign a multitude of documents, which will be compiled and given to you in a large folder of some sort. We normally have kept this folder separate from the day-to-day "working documents" of each property. At that point, you will naturally begin to incur daily expenses (and obtain receipts), accept rental applications, collect monthly statements, etc.

There are several key reasons that you want to make it a point to keep good records. The first is you want to be able to track profit and loss over the course of a month and year. Henry, who is very good about keeping records, has always kept a monthly ledger of each property, the rental revenue collected, and any expenses incurred during the month. At the end of each month, he can then very easily calculate the profit or loss overall and for each specific property. If we then want to calculate it for a given year, it is then very easy to do. Second, one must report all of these things to the IRS. There is a certain form, Schedule E, used to calculate rental revenues and expenses. Each property must be listed separately, rental revenue for the year reported, and then itemized expenses also taken into account, ultimately leading to the overall profit or loss for each property and the overall investment property portfolio. We have found that investment property is a good tax shield, as depreciation can also be written-off (although it ultimately must be accounted for when you sell the property). Mortgage interest can also be deducted, and you will receive a tax statement from each of your mortgage servicers listing the amount you paid in interest over the course of the year. If you are vigilant about keeping receipts, preparing your taxes (and being able to deduct the proper amount) is a relatively simple task.

9. *Learn the tenant/landlord law in your jurisdiction.* No matter how well you keep records, pay your mortgage payments, and try to get along with tenants, you will inevitably have tenants who test your patience by not paying rent on time. My own perspective is that if you feel that a late payment is a one-time occurrence and that they are generally good tenants, you might want to consider cutting them a little slack. This will save you a lot of time, energy, stress, and money. In fact, to file a notice for eviction with the Justice of the Peace can run between $75 and $200. However, if it seems it is a recurring incident and/or that they are trying to take advantage of you, it might be a wise idea to go ahead with the eviction process.

The first thing you must do is to have a firm date in the lease agreement of when the rent is due. Usually in the pre-printed rental forms available at stationary stores there will be a date already, but be sure to check it and know what it is. If they do not pay by this agreed upon date (as acknowledged by their signatures when they move in), you can give them a Three Day Notice, advising them that they must pay within three days or that you will proceed to file a formal notice of eviction. Usually this notice is enough to prompt them to pay, especially if it contains all the correct legal terms. If the tenants do not pay (or attempt to arrange payment with you), it is up to your discretion as to whether to proceed with the filing. You will need to do some research to find out exactly where you need to go in your area to file a notice of eviction, but this is the general framework.

Once you file the formal notice for eviction, the sheriff or Justice of the Peace will deliver a summons to them to appear in court regarding the matter. As I mentioned previously, there's a good chance that during this time tenants will actually move out, as not many want to go to court over it, especially since they know that they are in the wrong. I have had several tenants move out during this window of time between the filing and the court date, which is fine with me. By that point, I have given up on them as occupants and just want to start over with new tenants. If this is the case, you can simply contact the office that issued the summons, indicate the occupants left, and that you would like to drop the case. In fact, we have never actually had to go to court over an eviction. We have been close, but always been able to cancel the hearing because the tenant had moved out. Thus, although the eviction process can be relatively costly and certainly stressful, it is a tool that you as the property owner can and should utilize if necessary.

10. *Remember that with investment property, it's a marathon, not a sprint.* In order to make any kind of money

with investment property-- excluding "flips" and other high-risk deals, which I do not recommend-- you have to hold onto it for a minimum of five years, preferably longer. Henry and I have passed the seven-year mark as of this writing, and the ones we still own possess a decent amount of equity. So if your investment horizon is less than a minimum of five years, it might be wise to avoid real estate. With that said, it is then necessary to view the property rental business as a marathon and not a sprint. In other words, try to remain "even keel" over the weeks and months of owning a property and dealing with the inevitable challenges that arise along the way, such as finding the right tenant, dealing with repair issues, and speaking with the mortgage company. It's a good idea to remain calm whenever possible-- in my experience, there are very few true "rental emergencies." In other words, try not to let the day-to-day experience of owning rental property get your stress level and blood pressure up, or you will never make it over the long-term.

Do you remember the story about our property that had the fire? Although it was quite a shock at first, I was impressed with how calm Henry was during the entire process. This in turn made me feel more at ease. If you have a good dwelling insurance policy on your property, you really have very little to worry about. Although you can always have a major plumbing issue, which potential property owners seem to have a tendency to focus on for some reason, there is really very little chance of this happening in real life. One can always simply cut off the main water supply located in the front yard of most properties. The other big potential scare that potential property owners usually have is dealing with tenant complaints. They feel intimidated by them and feel that they won't know how to handle them. Although initially we struggled with this, one can easily overcome the issue. We have always encouraged tenants to take an "ownership perspective" of the property-- in other words, to treat it as their own home instead of something they are just renting. This has worked wonders. The other piece of advice I can offer is to do your best to keep your tenants happy, but remind them that the rental business is a *business*, and although you'd love to fix the house to look brand new, you always have to watch expenses and make sound business decisions. In other words, if they want a brand new house, they should *buy* a brand new house and not rent one.

My objective has been to give you an idea of the nature of real estate and how to benefit from it. Although I will be the first one to admit that it is not for everyone, it is a way to generate wealth if you have the right temperament and at least five to seven years to allow your investments to rise in value. However, before you delve off into the world of real estate, do your homework. Read anything you can get your hands on, listen to courses, speak with local investors and realtors, and even ride around to look at potential areas of town in more detail. If you then decide that real estate investment is right for you, at that point you'll have a solid foundation upon which to build.

Chapter IV
Retail

By the end of 2007, I had begun divesting of some of my larger real estate holdings. In November of that year, I had sold my commercial building in the Florida Panhandle after months on the market and for somewhat less than what I was hoping. I loved the autonomy and feeling of independence that came with being my own boss and running my own business, but I increasingly began to feel the need for something a little more conventional, such as a retail type business. My experience earlier in life in the retail business as a sales associate and the success I had during those years had planted the seed in my mind that a retail store of some sort might be a good fit for me.

In fact, while I was in Florida finalizing the sale of my building, I began to look on the internet for businesses for sale. I came across several that seemed interesting to me and started making phone calls. I really didn't know exactly what I was looking for, so it was sort of a "shotgun" approach for a couple of weeks. Normally a business broker lists a business for sale, which is who I dealt with initially for each respective business about which I called. I then narrowed it down to about three or four businesses that I thought had potential-- a couple of jewelry stores scattered around San Antonio and one or two other miscellaneous businesses. I had a couple of conference calls with the broker and actual business owner for each respective business and was able to ask questions about their business in general and obtain any financial statements they allowed me to have. Although each of these businesses had potential, none really captured my attention at that point. After looking around for a few more weeks, I came across another jewelry store for sale for what I considered a reasonable amount. I considered this a fair price since some of the other businesses I had been inquiring about were on the market for several times that price. However, there was one more thing that caught my eye; this one was located in a unique place-- the San Antonio Riverwalk.

In case you are not familiar with the Riverwalk, it is the most famous tourist destination in San Antonio and arguably the most famous in all of Texas. The San Antonio River runs all the way through downtown, and about thirty years ago, the city started to design the accompanying Riverwalk-- broad, open boardwalks following the river with restaurants and stores all along what is now a several mile stretch. There are many wonderful hotels along the Riverwalk. In fact, San Antonio is a major conference hub these days, drawing in literally tens of thousands of conference attendees a year with almost any type of organization you could imagine.

I met with the owner, who was a Mexican national and had other jewelry stores in different locations throughout the city. I happened to be acquainted with him already because I had bought jewelry from him before at one of his other stores. Henry and I were still close business associates, and I asked him to be a part of the process as well-- something that he was happy to do. The storeowner, Rafael, had been selling more semi-precious stone jewelry at this location (as opposed to his other stores, where he sold primarily traditional gold and silver). He had several employees who ran the store for him. In fact, one of the first things that stood out to me was the fact that he barely seemed to spend any time at this store. He told me that he "popped in" a couple of times a week to collect money and check in with the employees. I remember thinking that this would definitely be something that I would change-- I would definitely be more "hands on."

As far as employees went, he had two girls who worked for him, Teresa and Marcia. It just so happened that they were cousins, so they lived together and often came in together to work. Teresa was the *de facto* manager, given that she seemed much more adept at the computer software and was very good at keeping track of inventory, labeling new merchandise with sales tags, inputting them into the computer, etc. I seemed to get along well with each of them and decided it would be wise to keep them on, at least for the time being. Although Rafael had informed them to a certain degree about the details of the sale of the store (such as when I would be taking over), I spent a good bit of time with the two (especially Teresa) getting to know their thoughts on the business, how we could best work together, what each of us could expect, etc.

After a few weeks of preliminaries, in early January 2008, we finalized the deal. The broker who had listed the business recommended a lawyer to assist me with the closing (to look over paper work and make sure everything was in order). The lawyer, Henry, and I met with Rafael at his own lawyer's office (who also happened to be his business partner in some other ventures). Rafael was a bit difficult to work with, as he had somewhat of a short temper and seemed to get frustrated when things didn't go exactly as he had planned. Although this made the closing a bit tense, it transpired without incident. I remitted the asking price to him in the form of a cashier's check, we signed all the necessary documents, and after about an hour, I became the owner of a new business on the Riverwalk!

After thinking about it over the months that followed, however, I began to wonder what the sales price was actually for-- there was probably only a couple of thousand dollars worth of jewelry on hand when the store transferred over to me and I would still have to pay rent every month. I concluded that this money was for the right to do business in that location and to have a basic business infrastructure already in place, which was especially beneficial for me since I had never owned this type of business before. However, I vowed that I would not pay this much for a business ever again, even though it was very nominal compared to the sales prices of comparable businesses.

I was excited, nervous, and a host of other things. However, I was also determined to make this business a success. After my real estate ventures, which had left me in a bit of a precarious situation due to the softening of the real estate market, I really needed this venture to work financially and I was prepared to do whatever it took to make it happen. I put a good bit more into the business over the subsequent months, as I bought much more and higher quality jewelry, bought new display cases, and decorated the store to make it more inviting to customers. Again, I felt that I had an advantage in the sense that I had worked retail before at some of the large department stores and seemed to have a good sense of style and presentation, which would definitely help me in the jewelry business, and I was prepared to work the business hard.

My plan was to work in the store as much as possible for two reasons. First, I would save on wage expenses since I would obviously not have to have an employee working my same shift, unless I needed her to do inventory or some other task that I didn't enjoy doing or quite know how to do. Second, I felt that I would be much better at sales than the employees would because of my retail background and the fact that it was *my store*-- I was not just an employee there to collect an hourly wage. In fact, when I looked at the sales revenue records while doing my due diligence, I realized that sales were rather dismal. As I mentioned previously, Rafael only came by a couple of times a week and actually never worked a shift there himself. He tended to work at his other store, which sold more high-end jewelry of gold and silver, and thus left Teresa and Marcia to their own devices. In fact, I believe that this was one of the main reasons that Rafael put the business on the market-- it wasn't making much money for him, although it was in a fantastic location. I always have wondered, though, how he expected it to make money if he was never there. It seemed to me very much of a "downward spiral" type situation.

My first order of business was to find a name for the business. As English is my second language, it is somewhat tough for me to come up with things like that-- things that require knowledge of the nuances of the language. After a while of pondering and throwing out names, Henry came up with "Thai Princess Jewelry." This struck a chord with me, and I decided immediately to go with it. The second order of business was to find an inventory source. Rafael had a bit of merchandise in the store already, which transferred over to me as part of the sale of the business. However, none of it was very pretty and seemed cheap. I knew this had to change in order for me to be as successful as I hoped. I also bought some inventory from him right before we had our closing-- Mexican silver with turquoise that was quite beautiful. However, after a while I realized that he sold it to me for too high a price. I never really trusted him about anything and knew I had to find a steady source (or sources) of attractive, reasonably priced jewelry.

I was going for the sterling silver/semi-precious stone type inventory, and the first place I found was a source in Thailand that I discovered while scouring the internet. I thought their entire inventory was reasonably priced, even with shipping and handling from overseas. Henry helped me the first couple of times until I felt comfortable with the exact type of merchandise that I wanted and was familiar with the ordering process. Besides this Thai source, I also bought things from other wholesalers around town, some consistently and some only once if I felt they were trying to cheat me in any way. Teresa was very helpful in the labeling of all the new merchandise, which was literally thousands of dollars worth. She also did things that I didn't want to do or wasn't capable of doing, such as working with the computer software to enter and record all of our new items. I spent a great deal of time down at the store those first couple of weeks, and overall I would have to say that it was a relatively "glitch-free" process.

Additionally, as part of the deal with Rafael, I also now had a little kiosk just in front of Thai Princess Jewelry, which I used to sell sunglasses. I appropriately dubbed it "House of Sunglasses." It didn't sell nearly as well as the jewelry, but I felt that it served two purposes. It added an additional source of revenue, even if it wasn't much, and it also served to catch people's eye and get them to stop and look at my merchandise. Once they were there, many times I could lure them into the jewelry store, which was a traditional storefront as opposed to just a kiosk.

The first couple of months were modest in terms of sales and revenue. I was getting to know the business and becoming acquainted with my employees. Besides Teresa and Marcia, I also had a couple of other part-timers, including another cousin of theirs. Although I had many years of retail experience, I had never owned my own business, so the process of running the store took some getting used to. However, I felt like I was picking it up quickly, and I enjoyed interacting with the tourists and conference attendees. The store hours were rather long, officially from 10 AM to 9 PM Monday through Saturday and 12 PM to 6 PM on Sunday, but I always tried to open a little earlier and stay open a little later. I felt like that gave me a bit of an edge on my competition.

Speaking of competition, very soon after I took over, Rafael and his partner opened another store very close to mine (probably about three hundred feet or so). This angered me because he had signed a non-compete clause as part of the sale. I asked him about it and brought it up to mall management, but to no avail. So from that point on, I was determined to out-sell their new store. I have always had a bit of a temper when I feel wronged, and this really got under my skin. I was determined to look for better merchandise, open longer hours, and undercut them-- in other words, to do everything in my power to drive them out of business. Another thing about me is that I've always risen to the challenge when someone has told me that I can't do something or in some way mistreat me. I felt very much betrayed, and I was determined to meet this affront head on.

One of my first major challenges after the first few weeks was dealing with employees. Although I had Teresa, who was very good at tracking inventory and keeping records, I quickly discovered she was not much of a salesperson. Marcia was not much of one either, nor were the other part-timers that I hired. So motivating them was a major undertaking. I also had to make sure that both the store and the kiosk had workers throughout the entire workday. This meant scheduling employees and eventually-- after Teresa's cousin left for another job-- trying to find and hire new employees. The primary way I went about doing that was simply to place a "Help Wanted" sign in the window. There was more than enough foot traffic to have people come in and inquire. The problem, of course, was to find *quality* employees. In fact, finding and hiring quality employees (ones who will show up on time, not call in sick, be able to interact with customers, dress appropriately, etc.) has probably been my greatest challenge of all since I opened. The lack of qualified, motivated employees out there is astounding.

The day-to-day routine of running a business, I discovered, was not that difficult once I learned the intricacies of it. I generally would arrive (and still do to this day) by around 9:30 AM, which was not incredibly early, but slightly before my competition and early enough to perhaps catch the folks that had an early morning flight home after attending a conference of some sort. I began to feel more comfortable with the layout of the store (which is very small-- about two hundred square feet) and began to arrange the jewelry and other decorative pieces in my own way. I had a few signs made up at the sign shop that read "Thai Princess Jewelry" and had art of the Riverwalk and other San Antonio attractions in the background, which I hung on several sides of the store. I also had several "sale" signs made up that read things like "*Sale-- All Merchandise 25-75% off.*" I've known since my retail days that the best way to entice potential customers to buy something is to make them feel that they are getting a great deal. In fact, almost all retailers do this to a certain degree, although I believe it's more prevalent in some industries (such as jewelry) than in others. My strategy since the beginning has been to mark up the jewelry to a rather high price then base the "sale" price on that. The retail industry involves a great deal of psychology, and a successful businessperson must be part amateur psychologist. So when a customer would get something at "75% off," that would usually still represent a very healthy profit for me.

Although I would spend about 70 to 80 hours a week at the store, I would normally have at least one employee with me during part of the day. For instance, Teresa could be working on labeling inventory and inputting the items into the computer while I spoke with customers and tried to make sales. That way, it seemed that each of us could perform the activity that we each enjoyed and was most proficient at doing. I have always made it a point to greet customers as soon as they enter the store and personalize their experience to the extent possible. Because there are so many other stores around that sell similar items, I have always thought that this personal touch is very important and helps to distinguish my store and gives customers a unique and memorable experience, especially if they are coming from out of town.

As the first few months went by, I began to get to know the other mall merchants as well as the security guards, janitors, and other mall employees. I've always considered it a smart policy to be on good terms with these types of people. For instance, I frequently receive new merchandise in large cardboard boxes. One of the mall employees in charge of trash pickup noticed this and that I was having difficulty disposing of all of them. Thus, he offered to come by when on his route, tear down the boxes and dispose of them for me. Naturally I was very receptive to that idea, and even though he didn't ask for it, I began tipping him a little for the service. You'd be surprised how far a relatively nominal sum goes toward influencing people and motivating them to act. This arrangement has seemed to work, and I continue to do this sort of thing with him as well as other mall employees who go out of their way to assist me.

Normally the months of January and February are relatively slow, and that first year was no exception. Although it's not necessarily that cold out, on many days it can be somewhat dreary. Thus, organizations tend to wait until closer to the spring to book their conventions. Therefore, it really wasn't until March when I began to see a sharp upswing in sales and realize what the store is capable of generating in terms of revenue. In March in south Texas, the weather starts to warm up dramatically, with many afternoons hitting the mid-80s in temperature. That first March was a good month, and I began to get excited about things. That's when we first began to experience days of high gross sales. I truly didn't know what the store was capable of when I bought it, because Rafael never did very much with it (he had been averaging roughly $10,000 a month in gross sales, which is not much at all). Although I believed that it had potential because of the fantastic location and my plan of working it myself as much as possible, I never would have been able to predict the extent of it. So when I started to hit my sales mark consistently in March and April, I became extremely excited. April is Fiesta in San Antonio, which is a weeklong citywide festival that is really the *de facto* start of summer. I was hoping that this time period would see me continue my sales streak, and I was not disappointed.

Around the end of May 2008, mall management asked me if I would be willing to give up my sunglasses kiosk, which as I mentioned, had been my sideline business located in front of the jewelry store. They told me that they would then allow me to sell my sunglasses within the jewelry store. Since my rent on the kiosk was relatively low, they were in talks with a potential tenant about renting it out to him for significantly higher. After some careful consideration, I decided to go ahead and agree to it. That would definitely help me to save on rent as well as make it easier for my employees to manage because they would not have to continuously walk back and forth between the two businesses to help customers.

As we began to move into summer itself, things really began to heat up (literally and figuratively). I realized that in order to have the store hours that I wanted, I needed more help. Besides Teresa and her cousin, I had hired other employees who were with me for different amounts of time (some several months, some only several days or weeks). I have always experienced high turnover with my employees, which is something that has always slightly vexed me, and I have given a lot of thought to. Possible reasons why this has always been the case are that retail tends to attract the kind of workers who frequently change jobs (it's tough to deal with customers) and the fact that I am rather demanding as an employer (much more so than most retail employees are used to).

During the summer of that first year, I was averaging about what I expected in sales. Generally, my profit margin on the items was around 70 percent; so after salaries, mall rent, taxes, etc. I was generating a healthy net profit. Things were going rather well to say the least. There seemed to be an endless stream of tourists and conference attendees. In fact, San Antonio is actually now one of the biggest professional conference destinations in the entire country due primarily to the Riverwalk. Although employee turnover persisted, I always had people coming in the store wanting to fill out an application, as I customarily had my "Help Wanted" sign up in the window. By the end of the first summer, I was firmly entrenched in the location and in the jewelry business. I had a product line that appealed to many people (turquoise and other semi-precious stones in the form of necklaces, earrings, etc.) and at a price point that most people could afford. In other words, it wasn't really a "big ticket" item for most people versus if they were to go to one of the national chains that deal in gold and silver, where a necklace can easily run $500 or more. Most of my merchandise was in the $20 to $60 range (although some went as high as $100 or so), so most of what I sold could be bought as a sort of spontaneous purchase. This could be as a gift from a boyfriend/husband to a girlfriend/wife, a woman buying something for herself while out with her friends, or an out-of-towner buying a souvenir for someone back home.

Although the vast majority of my customers were very polite and respectful of my shop, the merchandise, and me in general, there were several occasions early on where they were not quite so amiable. Most of the time the behavior would be something to the effect of sifting through my merchandise and asking if the items were "real." Although almost all of the merchandise I have bought over the last couple of years is genuine turquoise or other semi-precious stones, some could perhaps be considered of simply moderate quality. This is the type of merchandise that I normally sell in what I call the "popular" price range-- normally $30 to $60 for a two or three piece set (necklace, earrings, and maybe a bracelet). I pay a good bit less for the item(s) at the wholesale level, so if I sell it for $30, that represents a healthy gross profit. I feel that this is a good range to sell merchandise in because, as I explained before, it does not represent too much of a commitment on the part of the customer and it is more likely to be a spontaneous purchase. I have also always carried more expensive, higher quality merchandise that uses a higher grade of stone, but these would usually sell for $100 or more. That was actually quite inexpensive considering the cost of semi-precious stones. Thus, I have always thought that I have provided customers with the best of both worlds in terms of options.

Around October of 2008, I began to hear about a woman wanting to sell her gift shop. She was located on the other side of the river. My store is on one side, and just around the corner is a pedestrian footbridge, which connects the two sides. Hers was beside the ticket booth for the popular riverboat tour. The first thing that popped into my mind was that there would always be a steady stream of people close to the store. During the peak season, there can be a line of several hundred people waiting to take the riverboat, which is a 30-minute boat ride touring the river, with the "taxi driver" giving a narrative of the Riverwalk and that part of the city. Henry and I met with the woman one Sunday afternoon to get our initial impressions of the store dynamics and how it was operated under her ownership. She had run the gift shop for over 20 years and had been able to use family members as employees in the store. Her employee expense, therefore, had always been minimal. That was something that, unfortunately, I have never had much luck with since my family has never taken much interest in the stores I've operated.

When I visited her shop the next week, my first impression was that it was extremely dingy. The paint job looked like it was the original from 20 years before-- something she later confirmed to be true. There was not nearly enough lighting and had relatively little merchandise given the size of the store. However, this may have been by design, as undoubtedly she was trying to draw down inventory as the store was on the market for sale. Thus, my first impression was not really the best. One of the things that I did like was the fact that it had an upstairs work area, and she already had a desk, drawers, a lockable storage room for inventory, etc. The main thing that I thought it had going for it, though, was the location. This was probably the first thing that jumped out at me when I heard about her store. Overall, I thought the store had potential. Although Henry really wasn't in favor of it, due mainly to my difficulties up to that point in finding quality employees, he reluctantly went along with it. Although she initially wanted a hefty sum for the business, I negotiated her down to considerably less. After a few weeks of talking and going back and forth, we pounded out the details and had a deal.

I alluded to this before, but speaking of sales prices for businesses, something that has always mystified me is what truly is acquired when one buys a business like this. The new owner still has to pay rent to the mall (or the city, as was the case with this new business). When there is little inventory to be had, such as was the case with Rafael's business when I bought it from him and the new business just described, the question comes to mind, "Well, what am I getting for this sales price?" The previous owner provides you with a list of suppliers and any store furnishings to go along with the bit of inventory that is there upon closing the deal, but does that justify the sales price? Additionally, in businesses along the Riverwalk, where by my estimation 95 percent of customers are one-time only customers (tourists and other visitors to San Antonio), you are not really building up a client base. Thus, you are not purchasing any real name recognition or client base. It is just the right to do business in that location by operating something that you do not have to begin from scratch. However, starting a business from square one is an extremely difficult thing to do, so there is some value in buying one that is already up and running. However, to me that doesn't really justify a high asking price if the new "owner" really has no ownership interest or equity in anything.

Thus, in November of 2008 I now was the proud owner of two full-fledged Riverwalk businesses. This time around the closing went much smoother than when I bought Thai Princess Jewelry. I used a lawyer of my choosing that I had known for over a year and had already performed various business-related services for me. I felt much more sophisticated than the first time around; I felt like I had the upper hand, and it showed in my confidence level. With the low sales price, lower rent than what I was used to paying, and a store already somewhat stocked with t-shirts, Mexican-style ceramic pottery and other gifts typical of San Antonio, south Texas and Mexico, the store was already in relatively good shape. However, one of the first things I wanted to do was to brighten up the store with new lighting fixtures and more colorful displays. My learning curve was definitely going to be shorter than with Thai Princess Jewelry. After giving it some thought, I came up with the name TPJ Gift Shop. I suppose I was considering the gift shop to be an offshoot of the jewelry store, thus the name TPJ. It also made it much easier to remember.

The first couple of months were decent in terms of sales, to a large degree due to the Christmas season. As the ticket booth for the river taxi cruise was right next door, there was a constant queue of people close to the store waiting to take the boat ride, which was very popular in large part due to the reasonable price. Many of these people would duck into the store for a few minutes while their family members were waiting in line. It also gave me a very good reference point for customers that came into the jewelry store when I told them about my new gift shop.

Although my sales were moderately strong during the latter part of the year, New Year's, and All Kings' Day (which is also a celebrated holiday in Hispanic culture and represents the *de facto* end of the holiday season), when February came around, I felt that I could take a little time to fix up the store a bit more. In February of each year the City of San Antonio drains the downtown portion of the San Antonio River, which is what the Riverwalk follows. As one can imagine, with hundreds of thousands of visitors every year, the river is inundated with trash such as cups, bottles, and cans even though the vast majority of people are very respectful and would never litter into the river. Thus, there is little tourist traffic during that week in February, when the riverbed is literally dry for cleaning purposes. During that week I had the store painted with a fresh coat of white paint and some other touchups around the store. A fresh coat of paint is probably the "biggest bang for the buck" in terms of making a home or business suddenly seem fresher and cleaner.

By March 2009, I had now become firmly entrenched in the gift shop and things were going along reasonably well. I enjoyed having the upstairs area at the gift shop and had a computer as well as a microwave there, and was able to keep jewelry and other inventory in the locked closet. However, around that time I began to have an unexpected annoyance in the form of my next-door neighbor, a woman who also ran a gift shop. Although we sold somewhat different items, with just a bit of an overlap, I believe she felt threatened because I was very gung-ho about the business, and she was not used to having much competition. The previous owner didn't push too hard so perhaps didn't represent much of a threat to her. She complained on several occasions to the city, who owned those spaces along the river, that I was selling unauthorized items, things that she also sold, etc. My strategy for dealing with this was simply to be as nice to her as possible. In truth she was a reasonably nice neighbor and would chat with me on occasion about various things but sometimes could be quite a bother. She was mostly harmless, though, so I did not let it get to me, and I was never reprimanded by the city for selling something that I should not, so it was in fact nothing about which to worry.

About six months into having the gift shop, I began to experience a few problems on several different levels. The first was that of having enough employees to cover the two stores for approximately twelve hours a day, seven days a week. A corollary to that was to have enough *decent* employees to cover these hours. By "decent" I mean ones that have the ability and willingness to speak with customers (greet and make small talk with), have their own transportation, dress somewhat professionally, speak properly, were able to count money, etc. I have never thought that those were unreasonable things to ask of an employee, but you would be surprised at how difficult it is to find employees who possess these qualities and retain the ones that you are fortunate enough to find. Then again, if you've ever owned a business with employees, maybe you wouldn't be surprised. I would have employees work with me for a couple of weeks, or a month or two and then quit or never show up again and not even claim their last paycheck. Other problems included the old air conditioning unit, which was probably thirty years old, and the electrical system in the store. The city absolutely refused to take responsibility for fixing anything, even though the space belonged to them. It seemed ridiculous that I, the tenant, would be responsible for keeping the space running properly, especially with the "big ticket" items such as the A/C unit. I thought about what would happen if I required my own tenants in the rental houses to pay for all their repairs-- they'd probably pack up and leave in the middle of the night! However, I had no choice but to fix these things. I did not want to put a lot of money into the fixes, since I knew the space was not mine, so most of what I had done could be considered just "band-aids," like having the A/C unit charged with Freon or having the condenser cleaned.

During the spring of 2010, I began to think about selling the gift shop. Although I felt it had been a good experience, I never felt comfortable in that location and always felt that the store itself had a sort of "bad vibe" or negative energy associated with it. I cannot say what this might have been attributed to, but even my employees seemed to feel this on a certain level. I had made many acquaintances since the time I initially began operations on the Riverwalk and felt that I probably would not even need a broker to help me list and sell. They normally charge about 10 percent of the asking price as the commission, which to me is ludicrous. I had been talking to another business owner for a few weeks about it and he expressed interest, hinting that his wife and other family members could run it while he ran his other venture, a small bar.

We talked back and forth about it for several months, and then finally came to "brass tacks" as far as asking price, how he would pay for it, where we would close the deal, etc. I told him I knew a lawyer who had helped me on several occasions with business matters, and he was amenable to that. I set the asking price at several times what I had paid for it, with everything included (merchandise, display cases, the computer and credit card terminal, etc.). I thought this was fair since I put a great deal of "sweat equity" into the business to bring it up to standards. I think I probably could have asked for more, but I reasoned that I had made back my initial investment as well as daily cash flow since I commenced operations, so this was essentially pure profit. The closing went smoothly, and he in fact went down to the store to start operations that same afternoon. I agreed to stay on with him for a day or two just to give them some additionally training and talk him through the "ramping up" phase, which I thought was only fair and courteous to do. In fact, I wish Rafael had done that for me when I closed on the jewelry shop. Last time I spoke with them, they were doing fine and indicated that they had almost recuperated their initial investment. I was always impressed and slightly envious that they were running it truly as a family business, with the wife, his parents, and children all putting in time. This to me is really the best way to run an operation like this, as you do not have to worry about sub-par employees' antics such as calling in sick, thievery, etc. and any wages that you pay are literally kept in the family.

Nevertheless, as I am always on the lookout for opportunities, around September 2010 mall management offered me a space around the corner from the Alamo on a pedestrian thoroughfare. After looking at the space, I fell in love with it. It was huge- nearly 2000 square feet of usable space, a bathroom, several closets, enormous storage spaces, and even a back room in which to relax. The other thing that appealed to me was that it was already empty, so there would be no buying of an existing business with the accompanying sales price. In other words, I would just have to move in and start business. Actually, that's a bit of an over-simplification, as there was a good bit of fix-up involved, but after already owning two businesses and going through what I had been through with those, this seemed like a piece of cake. I recruited my son-in-law and some of his friends to help me paint, put in appropriate shelving, get the computer and credit card terminals running, stock the shelves, etc. By late October, I opened my doors for business. I was extremely pleased with how well the store turned out, and I even had display windows in the front that I could use to put mannequins in to display my t-shirts and hats. I would have to say of the three businesses that I had now owned on the Riverwalk, this one got up and running the fastest and the easiest. I suppose that should be expected, however. After all, once you learn the tricks of the trade, anything gets easier. In the year I have been open as of this writing, things have been going well. However, nothing compares to my original business, Thai Princess Jewelry, as far as gross sales and profit margin. It is much easier to make the "big money" when the majority of your sales are $25 to $50 apiece versus $5 or $6 as is the case in a gift shop.

As far as dealing with employees and keeping them motivated, I have always been willing to try just about anything, and it feels as if I have. I have always wanted to provide them some sort of incentive to sell, to do their best in talking to customers, and ultimately "move" merchandise. Although I have always considered offering employees solely commission-- which would be a generous percentage of the sales price, such as five percent-- nobody ever really wanted to take me up on it. I have offered that to Teresa and some of the others on several occasions, but Teresa especially was always averse to the idea, as she never was one to make many sales-- she would rather work with inventory and organize the store. However, I have had some luck with the idea of bonuses, which in effect have been somewhat informal or spontaneous type arrangements. For example, if we were doing well on a Friday or Saturday night, I would say something to the effect of, "Hey, if you can help me reach $1500 (in sales) tonight, I'll give you $10." This acts as a sort of challenge to them and usually has had quite a positive effect. Another thing I have done with some success, especially toward the end of the month, has been to offer a challenge such as, "You know, today is the 28th and we've sold *this much* so far this month. If we can make *that much* before the end of the month, I'll give you $25." It serves almost like a dare of some sort, with my throwing them out a challenge and seeing if they can rise to it.

Overall, I have had only one employee who has caused me any significant trouble. Although Monica was a very good salesperson, she was a trouble maker-- petty, jealous, and someone I never quite trusted to represent my interests at the store. I even had suspicions of her stealing merchandise on some occasions. Monica had worked on the Riverwalk for several years with different merchants and even had a sister who had been a long-time Riverwalk employee. Although Monica was a good salesperson, I always had hesitations about her. I overheard from other merchants that she would frequently pose as co-owner of the store. In other words, she would feign that she and I were business partners. She would also try to "stretch" her time sheet by milking as much time as possible out of the few minutes or so after her shift was over. For example, she would drag her feet when closing the shop at night and if she finished at say, 9:03 PM, she would write down 9:15 as her departure time. I would also find many items (especially the nicer ones) missing and began to suspect that she was lifting them to sell at flea markets on the weekends. At the end of her time with me, she began to be very disrespectful in the way that she spoke to me, once leaving several profanity-laced messages on my voice mail when I reduced her hours. After I ultimately let her go, she even filed a complaint with the state workforce commission, which I promptly refuted. Although I missed her as a salesperson, and even on several occasions over the next couple of years considered hiring her back part-time, I fortunately came to my senses each time and remembered how much heartache and trouble she had caused me previously.

The most recent challenge I've had has been with attempting to establish a website for my gift shop. I'm very aware of the power of the internet and the affinity that people have these days for online shopping. After weighing the pros and cons of designing a website, I decided to move forward with it. My main hesitation was that most of my customers are just "one shot deal" type customers. In other words, they are customers who are in San Antonio either on vacation or are attending a conference and just happen to stumble into the store. I most likely would never see them again. Furthermore, I wasn't quite sure if this type of merchandise-- such as t-shirts, mugs, Mexican pottery and other items that serve as souvenirs of one's trip to San Antonio-- would be the type of items that people would order on the internet after their trip was over (or people who just randomly happen to come across my site). Nevertheless, I decided to move forward with it.

The person who I hired to establish my website was not a professional web designer but someone I had met about a year prior when I listed the jewelry store for sale. He had actually been the business broker. He had since left the business brokerage firm and apparently was trying to get into the internet design business. At any rate, he asked for half the money upfront, which I hesitantly agreed to. After requesting several times for him to come down to the store to take digital pictures of the merchandise and his not showing up, I had to turn up the heat on him. I was finally able to pressure him to get the website finished, although not at all to my satisfaction, and reluctantly paid him the other half of what we had agreed. It was full of misspelled text, sloppy graphics, and blurry pictures. In fact, I have since "abandoned" the site, which in effect means that the website is no longer up and running. What's more, on a couple of occasions when he came to the store, he asked my employee on duty for parking money! He even called a month or two after he finished the website to ask if he could borrow a couple of thousand dollars to buy some software for his business! I politely declined, but inside I felt a great sense of satisfaction. I truly believe in karma-- in the old adage that, "what goes around comes around." The main lesson here is *not to do business with desperate people.*

Now that you have a background of where I'm coming from in my own retail business career and some of the challenges, successes, and failures that I've faced, in the next chapter I will share with you some thoughts and tips for being successful in a retail business.

Chapter V
Retail Tips

1. *Have a business plan.* A business plan can be as general or as detailed as you'd like. In my view, a more general plan gives you flexibility to change the tactical day-to-day approach as you deem necessary. However, a more detailed plan may provide you with more insight into what it is you actually are trying to accomplish, how you plan to go about doing it, the resources you have at your disposal, and the timetable you have allotted for yourself. It has been my experience, however, that if you plan to raise money through loans (either through a bank, the Small Business Administration, or so called "angel investors"), it is to your benefit to be as detailed as possible. Loan officers and other investors want to see that you have thought through your business plan as much as possible, planning for all foreseeable contingencies. If you are going this route, I think it's also beneficial to have it professionally printed and collated in the most aesthetic format possible. Color is better than just black and white. In other words, in your quest to seek outside financing, both content and presentation are important.

The main purpose of a business plan, regardless of whether you plan to seek outside financing, is to give you a "blueprint to success." You should identify beforehand the product or service you plan to offer, what makes you distinct from your competitors, who your target market is, how you plan to offer the product or service (with a storefront or over the internet), general expenses, costs vs. revenue, breakeven points for making a profit, etc. In other words, it should include a snapshot of the scope of the business and why you are undertaking it. A business plan is really a fundamental tool to success in a business-- I know of very few businesses that have experienced success over the medium to long-term that *did not* have one. I started with a more general business plan, as I wasn't quite sure of the scope of my business at the outset and didn't believe that I would seek outside financing

Ultimately, I did have someone to lend me money, but this is someone who I had borrowed from on many occasions over the years and with whom I had a very good standing. However, recently I have updated my plan to reflect my current business status and how I see things evolving over the horizon. That's the other thing to remember-- you can have a great business plan that you prepare at the inception of your business, and that plan may serve you extremely well. However, don't be afraid to "tweak" it as your business grows and evolves.

2. *Have adequate cash reserves.* This extremely important element will help to determine the ultimate success or failure of your business. There are hundreds of thousands of would-be entrepreneurs out there, many of whom I'm sure would be fantastic business owners. Does this mean that they should

all attempt to open businesses? Unfortunately, it does not. It is critical that as you ponder whether to take that ultimate leap of faith and open your "dream business" that you take stock of your finances. It is crucial that you be honest with yourself about whether you have the finances to back up your endeavor. Granted, it's not necessary that you have on hand all the money needed to get your business up and running and then to sustain it through those first months, but you must be able to get it from *somewhere*. In more technical jargon, you must be able to *secure financing*.

There are dozens of places you could potentially raise capital to start your business, but some of the most common places are bank loans, Small Business Administration (SBA) loans, personal loans from friends and family members and lastly, personal credit cards. Be careful with the last two options, however. I would recommend putting up as much of your own capital as you can comfortably handle, as this may lessen your financial burden down the road. It will also convince potential lenders that you have a large financial stake in the success of the enterprise. If you are interested in opening a franchise of some sort, there are literally hundreds of franchises out there these days offering products and services as diverse as fast food to educational and tax preparation services. Many times, they will offer some degree of in-house financing. However, even they will generally want to see the potential franchisee have a certain net worth and be able to put up a certain amount of personal funds.

Unfortunately, I have met many would-be small business owners try to get their enterprise off the ground with very little in the way of capital funds. In my opinion, this is a big mistake and one that virtually dooms your business endeavor to failure. Start a business only if you are financially able to not only initialize it and "get it off the ground," but also to sustain it and yourself (rent, food, family needs, etc.) for at least *six months* beyond that. In my opinion, one of the worst things that can happen to a business owner is to have a great idea, put everything on the line and spend a boatload of money to get the business running, only to run out of funds before the business turns successful. Be honest with yourself in this regard. Your financial future literally depends on it.

3. *Become familiar with all aspects of your business.* Although you as the business owner may enjoy one area in particular over all the others, it is imperative that you become familiar with all aspects of the business. That doesn't necessarily mean you will be an expert in everything, but it is vital that you have at least a working knowledge of all areas. For instance, I have always enjoyed the selling aspect, but I really don't enjoy doing inventory, and it's something that I avoid whenever possible. It's tedious, hurts my eyes looking back and forth between the computer screen and the items, and can eat up a tremendous amount of time. However, I've learned that since I am the business owner, I must know how to do inventory. I came to this realization the hard way-- I

would constantly get new inventory in, and on more than one occasion, Teresa would not be there to begin inputting it into the computer and labeling the items to put out on the shelves. Thus, one day I asked her to show me how to do it. I had to take notes (I always keep notebooks around for writing things down) so I could go back and reference it, because the whole process seemed to be incomprehensible to me at first. However, after a few times of doing it, I began to pick it up, and it started to make more sense to me. For you, it might be something very different; however, I am sure there is at least one aspect of your business that you do not necessarily like and given your druthers would prefer not to do. However, what would you do if the employee who usually takes care of this function for you suddenly quits? Are you going to allow your business to come to a standstill because of it? You as the owner must learn every aspect of the business, because it's your name on the line.

4. *Take care of your customers; they are your lifeblood.* This may seem obvious, and most business owners know this intuitively, but it bears repeating. Customers truly are the lifeblood, the backbone, the heart and soul, and every other similar metaphor that could be thought of when it comes to your ultimate success. Customers are what drive the business forward. This is especially true for the retail industry, where customer interaction is part of each transaction. Here on the Riverwalk, where so many customers are first-time visitors to San Antonio and/or Texas, the way we treat customers,

however brief the encounter may be, also has the potential to leave a lasting impression of the city or state. Therefore, in addition to being a retail merchant, you might also consider me an ambassador of San Antonio.

In the retail business, especially in a sort of "boutique" environment such as my jewelry shop, first impressions and the way we look, speak, and act toward customers is probably more important than in most businesses. Since jewelry is a luxury good, and by no means essential for people to buy, I try to keep this in mind as much as possible-- although it can be difficult sometimes to deal with customers on the Riverwalk (who can at times be a bit rowdy). In fact, I would go so far as to say that my treatment of customers has developed into a habit. In other words, as soon as the customer enters the store (or if I approach them outside the shop window if they happen to be looking in), I will greet them with an enthusiastic, "Hello, ma'am/sir, how are you?" I will then inform them of my current sales and ask them if there is anything in particular they are looking for. If they seem to be in a good mood and willing to speak, I'll ask them how they are enjoying San Antonio and what they have seen so far. It is in making a connection that I am able to make their experience here a memorable one. I always try to have a smile on my face because I know that the vast majority of people are out mulling around on the Riverwalk trying to enjoy themselves, and I want to play to that. In fact, if a customer walks in with a beer in hand-- usually the husband of the woman coming in to look around-- I may even offer them another. You should see how they light up when they hear that! I would venture to say that very few retail shops around town do that.

Many times things like this will loosen up the customers and put them in the mood to spend. This is especially true if it is a romantic couple of some sort, because in the vast majority of these cases the man is the one who will actually be paying for the item. Here is something else that I have discovered: many people like to shop when they are upset and have the desire to talk while they shop. Studies have shown that shopping releases "feel good" chemicals in your brain, which is why people like to go to the mall to shop when they are feeling down about something. In reality, the studies go on to say that the "feel good" chemicals are released just by looking for something to buy and that the actual act of parting with your money leads to a quick letdown, but most people don't consciously realize that. It goes back to what I alluded to earlier-- that shopping, in its purest form as a recreational activity, is meant to be a pleasurable experience. Even supermarkets have noticed that fact nowadays and have designed stores that are specifically designed to entice, educate, entertain, and mesmerize shoppers by the aisle design, cooking demonstrations, free samples of exotic dishes and product presentations.

I'm of the opinion that we, as small business owners, really need to create an *experience* for the customer as much as possible. This is especially true for owners who cater to more of a niche market and have more of a "boutique" atmosphere. Let's face it-- very few of us can compete with the likes of the mega-stores based solely on price. We must try to get them to remember the time they spent with us during that interaction. Many times people want to have an "experience" when they enter your business, not just feel like they're walking out with a lighter wallet and a trinket that they may or may not ever use. Make it special for them in as much as possible, because without them, you wouldn't have a business. If you do that, doors will open for you.

5. *Be a good neighbor in as much as possible.* Do you believe in karma? Not in the mystical sense, but in the sense best expressed in the phrase, "what goes around comes around" and the biblical adage of the Golden Rule-- "Do unto others as you would have them do unto you." I most certainly do. I believe in spreading goodwill for several reasons, many of them not entirely altruistic. Although I am indeed willing to help my neighbors (other merchants, mall administrators, tourists asking for directions, etc.) for the pure joy of assisting others, I do believe that eventually the good deeds will come back to me. It goes back to the old saying, "You scratch my back, and I'll scratch yours." I believe that if you treat others with respect and are willing to lend a helping hand whenever possible, eventually you will have a "credit due" whenever the time comes. Believe me, there will come a time when you need assistance. Again, don't help someone

simply because you are expecting something in return, but it bears keeping in mind that this is how the world works. I will help you this time and not expect anything in return; however, when I need help, I will also not hesitate to ask you for assistance.

Now granted, there is a mystical quality, something that none of us can quite explain, about what eventually happens to someone who is a "bad neighbor." You know the type-- the neighbor that always seems to be slightly conspiring against you in some way. I had co-workers like this when I worked as a sales associate in several of the large retail clothing chains earlier in my life, and I have fellow merchants and business operators like that now. However, it's amazing to watch what eventually happens to these types of people. Inevitably, the "bad vibes" that they were spreading at some earlier point will come back to bite them in some way. Consequently, I've learned not to wish misfortune upon anyone, because this negative energy will eventually catch up with me. What's more, there is no reason to wish misfortune upon anyone-- the pie is more than big enough for all of us. For example, we as Riverwalk merchants can all be successful-- it is not what economists call a "zero sum game." Again, the best advice is simply to follow the Golden Rule.

6. *Treat employees like employees, not friends.* This is such a difficult one for so many business owners, including me. In fact, I still have a hard time with this one. On more occasions

than I care to remember, I have had my feelings hurt by employees who have left unexpectedly, stolen merchandise or disappointed me in some other way. To be quite honest, employees *will steal* from you if given the opportunity. It is very hard to separate the personal from the professional and when we work with employees so closely for so long, we almost inevitably begin to develop a degree of fondness for them. I'm not saying this is wrong, but we as business owners must make a great effort to keep these feelings in check. This is especially tough for those of us who naturally like people and feel affection towards those close to us. I mean, when you work with someone day after day, week after week, month after month, it is easy to lose sight of the fact that you are *paying* him or her to produce results for you.

You might ask what is wrong with treating employees like friends. I suppose every business owner has a different take on this sort of thing based on his or her own experiences with employees, but my own experiences have led me to believe that employees eventually will take advantage of your kindness in some way. Many a time I have had employees call to say they wouldn't make it in on time due to family issues or had to leave early to catch the bus and thought I would understand. I am a kind-hearted person by nature, and it is very easy for me to be attached to people. Therefore, this idea of treating employees like employees and not friends is not something that comes easily for me. However, I have matured as a business owner and now am much tougher with my employees, and as a result lose less sleep at night worrying about whether to reprimand or fire an employee. In other words, I have now built up an emotional barrier between my employees and myself. Whenever I feel myself drifting a little too close to that imaginary line that separates employee and friend, I just think back to the experiences I've had over the last few years when employees have mistaken my kindness for naïveté or weakness. In contrast, I've seen employers bring food to employees, joke around with them, etc. In my view, this creates a dilemma for the business owner when he or she is forced to reprimand the employee. It will seem like you are trying to reprimand a friend or family member, and we all know how hard that can be. When emotional ties distract us, it compromises our positions of authority. In a similar vein, compliment your employees when appropriate, but don't go overboard. You have to be able to draw a line between complimenting them (ultimately to inspire them to work hard, be loyal and act in your best interests) and giving the *unwanted* impression that *you need them more than they need you.*

If you are like me and naturally have trouble separating employee and friend, just imagine them taking advantage of you in some way, laughing behind your back because you believed that they were truly sick, or something similar. Build up some emotion about it. Imagine the employees who you've trusted and with whom you've developed a connection stealing from you in some way or talking excessively on their cell phones when they should be helping customers. This is not to say that they would do that, of course. I always believe in giving them the benefit of the doubt with things like this. All I am saying is that imagining this kind of thing can help you to build up some natural aversion to wanting to become friends with your employees. I can guarantee you that they are not looking to be your friend. For the most part, retail employees are there to earn a paycheck with as little effort as possible and then get on with their lives. Treat them with respect, yes. Develop a friendship with them? Definitely not.

However, with that said, you also have to inspire your employees. Give them a goal or something to aspire to on a daily basis. For instance, I previously mentioned that I like to give my employees spontaneous goals. If we are doing well on a particular evening and are closing in on a big number-- let us say $1000 in gross sales to be a sort of tipping point between a good day and a great day-- I will say something like, "Hey, if we can reach $1000, I'll give you an extra $10." Incredibly, this spontaneous bonus is highly effective. Perhaps it's simply something innate within a person that likes an unanticipated challenge. All I know is this technique seems to work.

Also, teach them to have a positive attitude and be knowledgeable about the products. There's nothing more detrimental to the outcome of a potential sale than for the salesperson constantly to respond, "I don't know" to a customer's questions. On the other hand, being knowledgeable about a product is a sure-fire way to help close a sale, in large part due to the increased confidence level of the salesperson, which tends to shine through in the interaction with the customer.

Lastly, always be willing to give words of encouragement to your employees and those you meet. Many employees in these kinds of positions never have been the recipients of much encouragement in life, and are in desperate need of someone to recognize them for their achievements. In other words, the psychological component is almost as important as the financial component. Make employees feel that they are benefiting in all sorts of ways, besides monetarily, from working with you. Let's face it-- in most cases, the money that one earns as a retail salesperson is not a huge amount. It helps with retention, employee morale, and just the overall "vibe" of the day-to-day business if employees feel that they are being treated fairly and are valued as human beings.

However, despite your best efforts, on many occasions it will not work out with employees. Traditionally, the retail industry has always experienced high employee turnover. The hours are long, the workers have relatively little education, and many times, they will move on to another job if they are offered just a few cents more per hour. Now granted, sometimes you're happy to see an employee move on. In fact, in my opinion, it's better to let bad employees quit than for you to fire them. Firing an employee, besides being stressful for you as the employer, can place yourself in a position of being a target of revenge, be it in the form of frivolous lawsuits or violent acts against your person or your business.

7. *Know who your competition is and what they offer.* Although very important, this is something many entrepreneurs overlook or to which they do not pay sufficient attention. Knowing who your primary competition is, what they offer, how they offer it, and what their competitive advantages are is essential to long-term success. This intelligence gathering is something that large corporations have done now on a very sophisticated level for decades. Although a small business person probably would not have the resources (or need) for intelligence gathering on their competition at that high of a level, knowing about the details of their operation can only help you. If possible, pose as a customer yourself (if you don't think they will recognize you), look around, ask their sales associates questions to see what the level of customer service is, compare prices and merchandise offerings, etc. If you believe you would be recognized if you went personally, send an employee you trust. In other words, try to get the most detailed and accurate information possible on those businesses that represent your primary competition.

Once you have that information, you can price your merchandise accordingly. It is very possible that you are pricing your wares either too high or too low. You also become aware of their ambience, their level of customer service (and where you stand in relation) and how you compare overall. Contrary to popular belief, competition is actually a good thing for business owners. It forces us to push ourselves to make our businesses better. The ultimate goal for any business is survival and prosperity for the long-term. We must know our competition in order to help us achieve this objective.

8. *Create an inviting atmosphere for customers.* I'm a firm believer that shopping should be a pleasurable experience. Now granted, just the act of buying things actually releases "feel-good" chemicals in the brain. That's why some people feel addicted to shopping-- the "high" is similar to gambling or winning the lottery. So many times, we as business owners don't have to do much to get people to part with their money. However, it is also nice, and much to our benefit, to create an atmosphere that "facilitates" customers to part with their money. In other words, soothing music (I normally have some 1970s soft rock in the background), nice color patterns in the store, and the arrangement of merchandise are all things that one can do to improve the store ambience. Lastly, employees dressed appropriately and in a professional manner is something that cannot be overemphasized. We

want to create a relaxing atmosphere to enhance their decision to spend, or at least not get in the way of it.

This last factor is often overlooked but is something with which I have always had problems. I have had employees show up to work looking basically homeless-- slovenly dressed, bad breath, unkempt hair, and by and large looking like they don't care one iota about their appearance. I have even tried to bring some of my gently used clothing for several of my ex-employees to wear, hoping that this would help alleviate the problem and not give them any excuses to come into work looking so disheveled. However, to my chagrin, this has not helped. I've come to realize that people in general, and employees in particular, have to take pride in their appearance and look professional and well-groomed simply because they themselves want to appear that way, not because I'm asking them to (or threatening to cut their hours if they don't).

I have heard it said that you should dress for the job you aspire to have, not the job you happen to be in now. For example, even when I was in my early 20s and was cleaning hotel rooms or working as a convenience store cashier, I always took pride in my appearance. I did not have much money, but I always made an effort to be well groomed and have on clean clothes. During my career as a civil servant, in which I did everything from manage military base lodging to work in Facilities Management in a base hospital, I always took great pride in my appearance and wore dresses, nice heels and scarves. It made me feel good and boosted my confidence to hear how people remarked positively about my appearance and complimented me on it.

In sum, just remember that customers have many options on where they can spend their money-- or even to spend at all. This is especially true in today's marketplace where consumers are more sophisticated than ever before. In order to "assist" customers in making the decision to spend their hard-earned dollars in your store, you must do everything in your power to make the process as painless as possible for them and to provide an enjoyable shopping experience. This is accomplished through a welcoming atmosphere and professionally dressed and well-groomed sales associates.

9. *Try to watch costs, but not at the expense of hurting your business.* This, of course, is a very fine line to walk-- a true balancing act. I have always been very vigilant as far as what I consider extraneous costs go, such as not being forced to pay employees overtime or not buying merchandise that I do not need. This could also include very mundane things such as having a small microwave in the store so that I can bring food from home and then don't have to buy lunch or dinner in the food court (which besides saving money is really much healthier than eating the mall fare). However, I also am willing to spend if I think it will assist me in maintaining or growing the business. In other words, I am always on the lookout for new merchandise to buy, and usually am willing

to risk buying new merchandise if I think there's a good chance that it will sell for a nice profit. I think that the mindset of many business owners tends to lean heavily towards one end of the saving/spending spectrum. That is to say, they either refuse to spend any money unless it is absolutely necessary-- usually these types of stores look very barren and spartan-- or they are spendthrifts and spend money as if it were water. I believe there is a nice middle ground whereby you keep track of costs but are willing to spend in order to attract new customers and keep the ones you already have.

As far as record keeping goes, I would recommend using whatever system you feel comfortable with and think you can adhere to on a long-term basis. I have tried computer software programs to keep track of inflows and outflows of funds but have ended up gravitating back to the old-fashioned "pencil and paper" method-- I record the day's sales along with salary, cost of goods sold, and other pertinent information (such as sales tax, etc.). Additionally, the point-of-sale software that I use on my computer/cash register keeps track of daily, weekly, and monthly sales and comes in very handy as far as being able to keep track of my store finances. Thus, my advice is to just do what you're used to and feel comfortable doing. Don't let anyone tell you that a computer software program is inherently better than an old-fashioned method. Again, the objective is to be in business for the long haul, and you should track finances on a daily basis, so use something that you understand and can live with.

10. *Pay yourself first when you are paying bills.* To pay yourself first is the only way you will ever build up enough financial security to retire, regardless of how much your business earns over the years. It's so easy to look at your bank account and think, "I have this much money in my account, so I can buy that much inventory" or something similar. However much you may love your business (as I love mine), nobody can know what the future holds. It is therefore essential to not only save for retirement, but also to have a "rainy day" fund with enough for six to eight months of living expenses.

How much is enough to save? Rules of thumb differ on this matter, but I would say at least ten percent of your gross profit toward retirement (more if you are really dedicated to that idea) and another five percent to your "rainy day" fund. If you have debt, however, you should add in another five percent of gross profit a month toward paying that down. It's not hard to do once you get in the habit, because money you don't have is money you won't miss. When you sit down to write checks for your accounts payable (your bills), just write one out to yourself (or to your retirement fund) at the same time. You will feel a tremendous sense of freedom once you see your account balance grow. Additionally, you will literally feel weight off your shoulders when you have paid off your consumer debts.

There is unbelievable freedom in not owing people money and knowing that you have enough in your retirement and other investment accounts not to have to work if you choose not to.

Although the percentages that I've indicated above are important, it's just one part of the equation. The other large part of the equation is *time*-- the amount of time that you have until retirement. Have you ever heard of compound interest? In case you're not familiar with it, it's really just interest growing upon interest. Albert Einstein called compound interest "the eighth wonder of the world." Although this may be a slight exaggeration, it cannot be denied that compound interest is the only way that most of us as individuals can amass wealth. Hand-in-hand with compound interest is the amount of time we give our investments to grow and mature. To give you a simple example, let's say you invest $100 for a year at five percent interest. How much would you have at the end of that year? It would be $105 ($100 x 1.05). How much of the new sum is interest? In this case, it is very easy to see-- $5. What if we were to leave this new amount in our account for another year at the same interest rate? What would we have at the end of year two? We would have $110.25, with $5.25 of that now as interest. What if we were to leave it in our account for a third year? We would then have $115.76, with now $5.51 as interest. Do you see the pattern here? As time goes by, our interest is growing. Eventually the amount of time we leave it in the account will be much more important than the actual initial amount.

Here's an interesting anecdote about the power of compound interest. It is widely believed that in the early 1600s in present-day New York, Native Americans sold the island now known as Manhattan for various beads and trinkets worth about $16. Since Manhattan real estate is now some of the most expensive in the world, it would seem at first glance that the Native Americans made a terrible deal. Had they, however, sold their beads and trinkets, invested the $16 and received eight percent compounded annual interest, not only would they have enough money to buy back all of Manhattan, they would still have several hundred million dollars left over. That is the power of compound interest over time.

Now that you realize the importance of paying yourself first and the saving and investing that go along with it, the question of what to invest in arises. Although there are countless options for the public as well as specifically for self-employed individuals, I will touch on just some of the more well-known investment vehicles. The first is mutual funds. Mutual funds pool money from thousands of investors and buy shares in dozens (sometimes hundreds) of different companies. Therefore, each "share" of the mutual fund really is comprised of numerous underlying companies' stocks. Today there are literally thousands of mutual funds that invest in such sectors as consumer products companies, high tech, and natural commodities. Thus, there is a lot to choose from, to say the least. One of the major benefits of mutual funds is that you normally can open an account with very little money (usually $1,000 or less) and can make subsequent investments of as little as $100. This is one of the reasons their popularity has skyrocketed over the last couple of decades. I don't buy individual company stocks because they can be extremely volatile. Mutual funds, however, are comprised of many different company stocks, so the benefits of diversification (of not "putting all your eggs in one basket") start to apply.

If you are looking for a retirement vehicle, there are several good options. There is the Individual Retirement Account which comes in either the "traditional" or the "Roth" form. The difference between the two is that the traditional IRA allows you to deduct your annual contributions from your income, thereby lowering your taxes every year. The benefit of the Roth IRA is that, while not tax-deductible in the respective year, it allows you to withdraw your money tax-free. Currently, the minimum age to begin withdrawing your IRA funds (in either form) without penalty is 59½. There is still some debate as to which is the better option, and although it does vary depending on your situation, most financial advisors have argued that the Roth version is the optimal version for most folks. The current maximum contribution for either version is $5,000 per year for a single person and several thousand dollars more for a married couple. However, an additional item that the Internal Revenue Service allows is for those over the age of 50 to contribute up to $6,000 annually. This helps people later in life who are a little behind on their IRA contributions to catch up. Other retirement vehicles are the SEP retirement fund and the Keogh Plan. These are tools exclusively for self-employed individuals and allow you to put aside more funds for retirement every year. If you are interested in any of these investment vehicles, I would advise you to learn more about them through the internet or a financial advisor before you begin investing. If you already have one or more of these vehicles, remember to max out those yearly contributions.

So again, pay your suppliers, your employees and the rent on your store space. However, before you do any of that, pay yourself. As you know, time goes by fast and retirement is closer than you think. Your "future self" will thank you many times over.

11. *Be on good terms with your suppliers, but always be on the lookout for new ones.* Your suppliers may not be people who you normally think of as being important to your business. However, to find honest, ethical, reliable suppliers is as important to the long-term success of your business as any other stakeholder, such as customers and employees. Although it is not as "sexy" to talk about good suppliers as it is to talk about how to win over customers and have them love your product or service, it is vitally important.

Given that fact, it is always a good idea to be on the best terms possible with your suppliers. You should strive to be as polite and courteous as possible, pay promptly, and generally be a good customer (remember that you are *their* customer). However, that does not mean that you blindly accept their prices or are afraid to ask for discounts-- you should *always* negotiate with your suppliers. Additionally, always be on the lookout for new suppliers, just as they are always on the lookout for new customers. It is a good idea to have at least three or four good, reliable suppliers at any given time and always have your eyes open for new ones.

I have heard fellow business owners on more than one occasion state that they only have one supplier. When I would ask them about it, they would normally reply something to the effect of "Oh, but they're *so* great and they give me *such* fantastic deals." Well, that's all fine and good, but I have a couple of questions for folks like this. First, how do you know that they're giving you such great deals if you haven't seriously compared them with other potential suppliers? Second, what will you do if one day your supplier goes out of business? Businesses go under every day. If you only have one supplier, you will be left scrambling if one day you call to place an order and a recorded message comes on the line saying, "the number you have dialed is no longer in service." Thus, I recommend having a handful of good suppliers and always try to cultivate more. If you do, not only will you never have to face the situation that I just described, you also have the added bonus of being able to pit suppliers against one another to try to beat each other's prices. In other words, you can say to Supplier One something like, "Supplier Two is willing to give me a shipment of product x for only y amount. Can you match that?" That is always an advantageous position to be in, especially since no one wants to lose a steady, well-paying customer. You wouldn't, would you?

12. *Keep your financial life to yourself.* Here's a somewhat radical idea, but one that I strongly believe is true: money is always out there-- you just have to grab it. What exactly do I mean by this? Being an immigrant from Southeast Asia, I am very aware of what poverty is. Although we did have electricity in my home as a young girl, it was prone to blackouts and thus was not reliable. However, we did not have running water, so one of my main chores as a young girl was to fetch water from the town well for my family. When my experience in a refugee camp as a new arrival to this country is added into the mix, I can safely say that I am familiar with life with little money and few material possessions.

Since I have lived in the U.S., I have always been amazed at the amount of wealth that is in our society. This wealth, in my view, is accessible to anyone with a minimal amount of ambition. When I was a young woman cleaning hotel rooms on the beach, I was always impressed with the fancy cars that I would see in the hotel parking lots and the generous tips that some of the hotel patrons would leave me. When I worked with civil service, I was always impressed with the budgets that my particular department controlled; sums that seemed astronomical to me but that were really just a "drop in the bucket" in the big scheme of things. Now as an entrepreneur, running retail businesses and being involved in real estate for several years before that, I am amazed by the sums of money that I have been fortunate enough to earn. What's more, these sums have seemed to come to me with only what I consider a reasonable amount of effort. I am not telling you this in order to impress you, but instead to *impress upon you* that acquiring money is not an insurmountable objective. It is there for the taking with just a moderate amount of effort, a clear goal, and a strategy for attaining it.

However, with that said, I strongly urge you to keep your financial life to yourself, especially if you are doing better than other business owners are. Nothing good can come from flaunting your financial success, and you can very easily make enemies and create negative feelings this way. Since I opened my first store in January 2008, I have consistently performed well, averaging well above most other fellow merchants in gross sales revenue. I would go so far as to say that I earn two to three times what most business owners generate that sell very similar items. As I've described previously throughout this memoir, I believe that what sets me apart is my attention to detail, my customer service enthusiasm, and my work ethic (I'm there about 60 to 70 hours a week minimum, sometimes more). In other words, there's a reason that I've done so well-- it hasn't simple fallen in my lap. However, despite this, I know there are many fellow merchants/business owners in the mall and along the Riverwalk who are envious of my success, regardless of the amount of effort it has taken to achieve it.

I recognized early on that because of this envy toward me, I needed to be discrete in my dealings with other business owners and not "talk up" my success. I have tried to be unassuming in my day-to-day operations and in a sense "stay under the radar." However, despite my best efforts, word invariably has gotten out that I am one of the most profitable business owners-- if not the most profitable for my size-- along the Riverwalk. I observe other businesses as I walk through the mall, and I always try to have a keen ear to what's happening around me. What I see more often than not are struggling business owners, business owners who are only there for a few short hours a week (usually to drop off merchandise, collect any sales revenue money, or take a quick look around) and business owners who, while wanting to have *superior* sales, are not willing to put in *superior* effort. In all honesty, operating a business on the Riverwalk, or anywhere for that matter, is not really brain surgery-- but it is extremely hard work. However, although it is hard work, I truly enjoy being there and feel blessed that I have my business.

In sum, keep your financial business to yourself-- especially if you are successful (or more successful than your peers). If a fellow business owner asks you how things are going-- usually this is to try to glean information and not because they are truly interested in your state of well-being-- you can simply reply something to the effect of, "Things are all right, but they could be better." Don't let on about your financial affairs-- nothing good can come of it. Remember that people who smile to your face can also be plotting your demise behind your back. Look for friendship and camaraderie outside of the workplace.

13. *Always have your guard up.* When you operate a business, especially if it gives the appearance of being successful, con artists and scammers "come out of the woodwork" to try to take advantage of you. Most of these unscrupulous individuals actually justify it by thinking that you have so much, and they have so little (and that they were given a "raw deal" in life) that they should be able to steal from you-- almost like you've done something wrong to be in the position you're in.

When approached by individuals offering you services and purporting to have your best interests in mind, be wary. Be polite but also be aware of ulterior motives. Ask for references, written material, check out their physical location, etc. Better still is to do business with only reputable firms-- forget the "fly-by-nighters" even if they promise you a lower rate. A corollary to this idea is to be careful about lending money-- even if they're friends, they probably won't pay you back. I've lent money to people over the years that came to me with tears in their eyes, promising to pay me back in just a few weeks with a healthy amount of interest. I have been approached even more since I have been a small business owner. I can honestly say that I've only had people even *attempt* to pay me back less than half the time. In fact, not long ago I made a vow to myself never to lend money to anyone again. Here's a tip-- if you decide to lend money, for whatever reason, just consider it a gift. If they pay you back, that's great. If they don't, you had already mentally written it off anyway.

14. *Hold yourself to a higher standard.* Being a minority, sometimes people say things to me such as, "Why don't you go back to your own country?" or, "You Asians are taking away all of our business." However, you have to keep smiling and tell them that this is *your* country too. Many people, regardless of how much you read and hear about the progress that we as a country have made in terms of racial and ethnic tolerance, still feel jealous toward successful minorities. I feel this is especially the case if one is in a situation similar to mine, coming into contact with people from all parts of the country and all walks of life for only one brief encounter. In other words, they would never have to face you again or the consequences of a mean-spirited remark. When you add alcohol to the mix (as there are many restaurants and bars along the Riverwalk, many people drink

a good bit when they are there), you have people saying things that they probably would not say otherwise. Now granted, most of the people I come into contact with are great folks, with kind things to say and just looking to have fun with their family and friends, but a significant percentage-- maybe two or three percent-- are malicious.

Although I take great pride in my Thai heritage and background, I consider myself an American. I became a naturalized citizen in 1976, and I have not even visited Thailand since 1995. Although I have a cadre of Thai friends and acquaintances in San Antonio and sometimes attend the Thai temple in town, I am fully assimilated, as I feel all immigrants should make an effort to be. I interact with everyone else-- including my children and other family members-- in English and make an effort to be an ambassador for both cultures.

In sum, my view is that if you are a minority and/or immigrant, you have to hold yourself to a higher standard than people who were born here. This is especially true if you look somewhat different from the "typical" American and/or have a strong accent, both of which describe me. In other words, I try to be extra kind, extra law-abiding, and extra careful in my dealings with stakeholders (customers, suppliers, and mall management). Again, I have always found the vast majority of folks to be very accepting of immigrants and other cultures, but there will always be people who resent you for being here, especially if you seem to be more successful than they are or are otherwise "taking jobs away from people that were born here." My advice is to greet these people with a smile and send out a good thought on their behalf. Then go back to making money.

15. *Be ethical in all of your business dealings.* I saved this one for last because I feel that it is the underpinning of all the others. It is supremely important to act in an ethical manner at all times with your customers, suppliers, employees, and any other constituents that you meet. Sure, in the short run you might feel like you're coming out ahead by "bending the rules" or acting in a dishonest or unethical manner. Granted, it is a temptation-- I also have been tempted to behave unethically over the years. However, in the end, acting dishonestly or unethically will only come back to haunt you. In other words, do not write bad checks, stiff your suppliers on their bills, etc. Besides being unethical, things like writing bad checks are actually *felonies* in many states-- in other words, you could possibly go to jail for writing a bad check. Is that risk worth saving a few dollars in the short-term? In my view, the answer is absolutely not.

If you want some real life examples of big name corporations that can trace their demise to the unethical dealings of their executives, look at companies like Enron, Arthur Anderson, Tyco and WorldCom. These companies were considered among the elite in their respective fields for many years but were brought to their knees in short order by the unethical dealings of a select few (their top executives for the most part). Thus, my advice is to take the long-term view and always act in an ethical manner. If you're not sure if something would be considered ethical or not, just ask yourself the following question-- would you like your actions to be on the front page of the newspaper?

Chapter VI
The Message

Now I'd like to shift my focus a bit and begin to describe to you some general principles that will assist you in the attainment of any goal you have in life, regardless of what it may be. I feel that the following lessons will go a long way in helping you to live a prosperous, fruitful life, regardless of the direction your destiny takes you. These are lessons I've learned through my life via personal experiences and things I've read over the years that I've tried to apply in one form or another.

Lesson 1-- *Know what you want.*

As we all know, we have limited time, resources, and energy. Therefore, we have to know what we want in our professional and personal lives. If we don't know what we're after, our brains don't have anything to "grab onto" -- there's nothing guiding us. However, if we have a clear mental image of what we want, or even write it down in a place where we can see it often-- at least once a day-- then we stand a much greater chance of success. For me, that "something" was having my own business. Even when I was cleaning motel rooms, I knew that I was supposed to do something bigger. At that point in my life, I wasn't sure exactly what that "something" was. As I grew older, I began to hone exactly what it was that I wanted, and began to have a sharp, well-defined mental image of what I wanted for myself. My ambition eventually drove me to real estate and then owning several businesses on the San Antonio Riverwalk. Although I have never been one to write many things down (written English has always been difficult for me), my clear mental vision of what I wanted filled me with ambition and drove me to eventually realize my business ventures.

To know what you want provides your mind with a "final destination." In other words, although you might not know exactly *how* you are going to achieve the particular result, you do have an "end game." It's similar to when you start out on a road trip. Most of the time, you have an end destination, a place that ultimately you would like to end up-- for example, New York City. You pack up your car, fill up the gas tank, and start toward the "Big Apple." Even though you may not know exactly how you're going to get there, you most likely will arrive at your destination. Along the way, you look frequently at your map, keep an eye out for the road signs and maybe even get lost a couple of times. The important thing is that you know what your outcome is-- what you ultimately want to achieve.

We all want money, love, and to feel important. However, each of us values these things, along with many more, differently from others. In fact, we ourselves will value these things differently over the course of our *own* lives as we mature and our priorities change and expand. It is all right to have an objective or goal at one point in your life and then several months or years later look back on that and think, "I don't want that anymore. It's not important to me anymore." There's nothing wrong with that. I can remember that happening in my own life on many occasions. If this happens to you, just ask yourself, "What's important to me now? What are my goals at this point in my life?" You then re-evaluate and continue moving forward. Don't feel "married" to a goal that doesn't make sense to you anymore.

With that said, however, don't let yourself "off the hook" for not following up on something that is still truly important to you. Ask yourself why you haven't made more progress on it. Is it because you spend too much time with activities that add little to your life, such as excessive television? On the other hand, is it because your family has required more time of you? I am a big believer in family, and think that sometimes there are legitimate justifications as to why your goals get off-track, but be honest with yourself. If you need to make changes in your daily schedule to accommodate your goals, then do it. If you find that you're more of a morning person than an evening person, then schedule time for accomplishing goals in the morning. Always try to give priority to your goals- allocate time for them before you allow yourself time for anything else. Just know yourself, know your body, and be honest with yourself as to your own mental and physical strengths and weaknesses.

Lesson 2-- *Become aware of your thoughts.*

Our thoughts are our most powerful source of energy-- more powerful than food, drink, or sleep. As Buddha said, "What we are today comes from our thoughts of yesterday, and our present thoughts build our life of tomorrow. Our life is the creation of our mind. Your worst enemy cannot harm you as much as your own unguarded thoughts. But once mastered, no one can help you as much" (www.thinkexist.com/quotes/buddha). Another quote that I have always liked is from Shakespeare, "There is nothing good or bad, but thinking makes it so" (www.enotes.com/shakespeare-quotes). What do these insights tell us? To me, they indicate the tremendous importance of being mindful of the thoughts that pass though our conscious and subconscious beings.

Have you ever heard the proverb, "You are what you eat"? Well, I firmly believe that we are what we *think*. Whatever thoughts our minds consistently produce become our physical reality. I don't think anyone fully understands just how this can be true, but if you listen to the life stories of the most successful people in any aspect of life, you will undoubtedly come to believe that it *is* true. The nineteenth century Dutch psychologist and philosopher Soren Kierkegaard said it very succinctly, "Our life always expresses the result of our dominant thoughts" (www.quotationsbook.com/quote/38942). Have you ever listened to or read about the life story of a movie star, professional athlete, singer, or any other celebrity who you admire? Invariably one of the common themes in all of these types of stories is that for many years their dominant thoughts revolved around being successful and making it big in their chosen profession. They "ate it, slept it, and drank it" for many years before they actually hit it big or were "discovered."

Have you ever caught yourself being in some sort of mental "funk"? If you're honest with yourself, what is the underlying cause of this in a vast majority of cases? It usually has something to do with your thoughts-- the way you represent things to yourself (in this case, it would be negatively). If you are in this mental state, you tend to have primarily negative thoughts long enough to change your mental outlook on life and probably enough to even change your physical sense of well-being. Yes, I believe that thoughts are powerful enough to physically change how your feel; your body chemistry is literally altered. If you do not believe me, think about the following question. When we begin to think about our children misbehaving, or dealing with a problematic employee-- envisioning the worse possible scenario-- how does our body react? Can you feel your heart begin to beat faster, your blood pressure start to rise, and perhaps your head begin to throb? Why would that be unless thoughts literally have the power to alter our physiology?

Lesson 3-- *Begin with the "end in mind."*

I have used this technique over the years, consciously and subconsciously, for both large and small goals. Although I think we all are familiar with this on an intuitive level, it's something that I've seen expressed in the popular psychology literature as well. This puts forth the very simple (but extremely powerful) notion that when you have a goal, long-term or short-term, think about your end result-- be "end result oriented." Then work backward from that point to help determine what should be done on a monthly, weekly, or daily basis to achieve the result.

For example, I recently was watching one of the many talk shows found these days on cable TV. The host was interviewing a very popular actress from the 1970s who has been at the forefront of the "anti-aging" movement over the last 15 to 20 years. While now probably in her late 50s-- which is by no means old, especially by today's standards-- she described her philosophy toward successful, healthy aging. She described how she started with the "end in mind"-- in this case, living into ripe old age with energy, health, and vitality. With that image serving as her mental benchmark, she then could work backward to help determine what she should eat, how she should exercise and what her other lifestyle patterns should be on a yearly, monthly, weekly and daily basis to help her achieve that end result of vigor into old age. Thus, for example, when faced with the temptation to eat fast food, or a very rich dessert, she could actually think to her end goal and ask herself, "Will eating this dessert help me achieve my end goal or detract from it?" This is a very useful technique indeed-- one which helps us to be mindful of what is ultimately of importance to us.

Of course, not every decision that we make in life is as all-important as how well we age. Most of the daily decisions we make have to do with things like business meetings, how to get along better with our children, how to keep the spark alive with our spouse or significant other, etc. However, we can begin with the "end in mind" here as well. For instance, if we have a business meeting with a potential client, we envision what it is we want to get out of that meeting-- what we want the result to be. If we are meeting with a potential client, obviously we want our result to be that this person becomes a regular customer. At that point, we can work backward to help us determine how we need to carry ourselves or what points we need to emphasize in order to achieve that result of gaining the client. If our result is to have an exciting, vibrant relationship with our spouse, we can then envision what we would need to do to make that happen. For instance, have date nights, commit to being intimate a certain amount of time per week, etc.

I would like you to stop right now and pull out your "success notebook" (you have one, don't you? If not, go out right now and buy one!). Now I'd like you to think of some goals that you currently have for your life, both short-term and long-term, of critical life importance and goals that may have lesser importance. Try to be as clear as possible as to what your result will be for each of these goals. For example, if one of your goals is to have a mountain cabin, try to be as specific as possible as to the size, location, and other specifications of the cabin-- that's your end result in this case. From there, begin to work backward. If this is a ten-year goal, describe what you would have to do on a yearly, monthly, weekly, and daily basis to achieve that. Where would you be in the achievement of your goal at the five-year point? It's useful to have these sorts of checkpoints so that you can make adjustments in your actions if necessary.

Again, begin with the "end in mind" in your large, life changing goals as well as your smaller, more short-term goals. I think you will find that this is a useful technique and something that will assist you in being mindful of what is truly important to you as an individual so as not to be "hung up" on life's daily trials and tribulations.

Lesson 4-- *Envision what you want & make it real.*

This builds off the previous lesson and is something I learned a long time ago that seems to yield almost mystical results. I can't explain how it works-- all I know is that it does work, almost with supernatural precision. It's actually "seeing" what you want to happen in your mind's eye before you undertake something. Psychologists call this act "visualization." It's something that for decades I've heard of professional athletes doing. I've heard them in interviews say things like, "I sit down a few minutes before the game and just envision myself throwing the ball where I want it to go." To use a current example, one very well known professional golfer has spoken very openly about how he uses visualization to imagine the ball being sunk into the hole before he actually putts it. Another example is that one of the most famous bodybuilders of all time would actually sit down before a competition and imagine himself hitting all of his poses sharply and blowing everyone else off the stage. Therefore, the concept is not new to athletes, but I believe using this concept is not something most of us think about doing in our daily lives.

When we visualize ourselves experiencing exactly what we want to have happen, I believe it sends our brain "directions." It makes it clear, beyond the shadow of a doubt, that *this* is what we want to occur. It goes back to the power of thought also-- I believe thoughts are entities and that they emit energy. Thus, when we envision what we want to have happen, in as much clarity and detail as we can, I believe this helps to set in motion events that will actually lead to its fruition in the physical world. How does this work exactly? I don't really know-- all I know is that it does work. Ask any athlete, actor, salesperson, or other professional who is forced to "rise to the occasion." They may not have realized that they're doing it, but I can almost guarantee they have included the power of visualization in their routine at some point or another.

Here's an activity: I'd like you to pinpoint a goal that you've had-- it could be to lose a specific amount of weight, garner the courage to speak to someone you've admired, take the first step to start a business, or whatever it happens to be. Then I'd like you to imagine yourself actually in the process of obtaining this goal. Try to include as much detail as possible, using as many of your senses as possible (sight, sound, touch, smell, etc.). Let's say your goal is to make a wonderful sales presentation to a potential client and have the client subscribe to your offerings. Envision yourself, again with as much detail and clarity as possible, making an irresistible presentation to that person, being as convincing as you've ever been, with confidence brewing over, and then having the person become your client. Imagine your self-confidence being magnetizing, with your skills of persuasion leaving the client no choice but to avail herself of your services.

When you do your visualization exercises, it's important to bring in as many senses into the picture as possible. Truly *feel* yourself shaking hands with the new client, *see* the colors in the tie you're wearing when you make that big presentation, or *sense* the wellspring of confidence as you step onto the golf course. If you desire a new job, proceed to list that job on your resume as though you already have it. Envision your business cards with your new title and company printed on them. Again, I cannot explain exactly how or why this kind of thing works, but why question success? Here is more proof of how this kind of thing is used in the real world. A recent professional football coach who was with his team in the Super Bowl decided the night before the big game to go ahead and get his players' fingers measured for their Super Bowl victory rings! He didn't wait until after the game was over and in the history books. He was confident in his team's ability the next day, and more importantly, undoubtedly he wanted to give his players the feeling that they had already won the game. He understood the power of visualization and making something *so real* that your brain has no choice but to make it come to fruition in the physical world.

Here is another example of the power of creating the future through visualization-- why do you think car salespeople allow you to test drive a vehicle? One reason that they're so eager for you to take that "first spin" is so your senses can visualize how it would be to own that vehicle. There's the "new car smell," the freshly washed and waxed vehicle with shiny tires, the beautiful untouched leather upholstery and the dashboard full of exciting new gadgets. All of your senses are engaged-- sight, sound, smell, touch, and hearing. You imagine what it would be like to own that car, probably without actually consciously realizing it. The salesperson intuitively knows that if he can get you into taking a test drive, his odds of selling you that vehicle increase many times over.

Don't underestimate the power of the mind to give you what you want. Give it a clear picture, using as many senses as you can. Do this at least once daily, preferably more than once. You will be astounded as to how quickly your visions of what you want are attained in the physical world.

Lesson 5-- *Focus "like a laser beam."*

There's just so much that vies for our time and energy on a day-to-day basis. I mean, we have commitments with our jobs, families, friends, and social organizations. So how can we possibly have time to accomplish the goals and objectives that we set for ourselves? One way to accomplish this is to give "laser like" focus to our goals. Obviously, this requires us to actually *have* a clear vision of what our goals are and consistently keep these goals in the front of our minds. In other words, we do something every day to bring us closer to our goals-- whether that is making a phone call, writing an email, reading about something in particular, or simply practicing a skill or technique.

We've all heard the analogies about the rock mason, who diligently taps away at the rock, day after day, thousands of time. It might seem that the artisan is not making any progress, because on the outside, that seems to be the case. However, those "little taps" on the rock are adding up-- the net effect will soon appear. Suddenly, after thousands of small actions on the part of the rock mason, the rock splits open. What if the rock mason were to have stopped just one "tap" too soon? The rock would have remained intact. It is very similar to someone drilling for oil-- if the driller stops just one foot too soon, the oil will not be found, and the precious resource will remain hidden. Therefore, the lesson here is to keep going, even though it seems that no progress is being made. We have to remember that small actions, done consistently, add up.

So what does this mean on a practical, real life level? To me it means that you should be doing *something every day* to reach your goal. Have you heard the proverb, "Every great journey begins with the first step"? I firmly believe that even the most daunting projects or goals seem more achievable once you take that "first step." A corollary is that every goal is attainable if you take small, incremental steps on a daily basis. In other words, every goal, whether it is losing 50 pounds, starting a business, or saving $10,000, is best achieved by taking direct, measurable action on a daily basis. For example, as I was pondering the best way to write this book, I was quite honestly unsure as to how I could get it done with all the other time commitments I have-- running multiple businesses, family priorities, etc. Thus, my strategy was simply to commit to writing one page a day. I thought, "That's doable-- I can manage that." At that point, I began to get excited about actually finishing the book and could begin to make headway on it. As I write this, I can tell you that despite my other obligations and time pressures, I have been able to keep my commitment to this seemingly small, but steady goal. I challenge you to do the same thing. Think of a goal that you have perhaps been putting off because you didn't think you had the time or energy to see it through to completion. Is it committing to that weight loss goal? Starting a home business? Learning a foreign language? It really doesn't matter-- the principle of "taking small steps" works equally well regardless of what the particular goal is. Let's suppose it's learning Spanish. Could you commit to 15 minutes a day of study? I'm rather certain if it's a goal worth pursuing and one that's important to you, you could find that amount of time each day. Although this quantity seems insignificant, if done on a daily basis, the results will begin to add up. However, hold yourself accountable-- don't let a day slip by without your 15 minutes of study.

If you think about it, that's how a laser beam works-- it's concentrated energy, just a thin beam of light. However, if focused on the same point for extended periods, regardless of the material, it will literally burn right through it. This is how we should be with important things in our lives. Focus on them, commit concerted effort and energy toward their attainment, and very quickly you will begin to see results. Let me be the first to extend the challenge. Commit to a goal you truly care about, break it down into small "steps," be diligent in the pursuit of those small steps, and watch yourself get closer and closer to your once daunting, but now very achievable goal.

Lesson 6-- *Be willing to work hard and sacrifice.*

It's no secret that to be successful, a person has to work hard. However, sometimes what seem like the simplest things are the hardest with which to follow through. I have always worked hard-- it was something that from a very young age was a necessity of survival. Later in life, I found that it was something I actually enjoyed doing. I mean, it's nice to sit down after a hard day's work and say, "Wow, I really accomplished something today."

When I opened my jewelry store, I knew that it was going to be hard work, but it turned out to be much more than I ever expected. Besides being on my feet for ten to twelve hours a day, six days a week, I had to make hiring decisions, locate merchandise, deal with suppliers, and perform other tasks that the owner/operator of a small business has to do. So really, it was more like eighty hours a week when it was all said and done. If an outsider looks at it like that, just on the surface, he or she would tend to think, "That's too much, it's not worth it!" However, I have not thought about it like that. You see, to me, it's my life, it's what gets me up in the morning, it's what "revs my engine." Not to mention that it has been very lucrative financially, which is an added bonus. I've learned over the years that big projects, like starting a business, many times need a lot of momentum and energy to get off the ground, but then once they are running, they don't need nearly as much energy to keep them going. It's almost like an airplane-- when it's taking off, it needs a great deal of momentum and energy to get off the ground, but once it's up, it takes much less to keep it in flight.

In all truthfulness, if you are pursuing something that you actually have identified as being important to you, as being a "goal" in the true sense of the word, the hard work involved should not be an issue. In fact, it should not really be considered "hard work," as to me that has a slightly negative connotation. Have you ever heard someone speak of a "labor of love"? This is a beautiful idiom, but what does it mean? Although there will be effort it is not drudgery. It's something that uplifts you, nourishes you, and makes you feel that you are accomplishing something worthy. There are many things that I can think of in my own life that could fall into this category, including the writing of this book. For example, I still put in full days in my stores selling to customers. I do this for several reasons, including the fact that I feel I have a much better handle on how to treat customers than many of my employees. After a full day of talking with customers, explaining merchandise and negotiating prices, I'm exhausted. However, it is a different sort of exhaustion, almost like a "blissful fatigue." In other words, I go home feeling good about the day, about what I accomplished, and the value I provided to my customers.

What if you could motivate yourself to do things you previously dreaded doing? Wouldn't that allow you to achieve things you previously thought unachievable? If you stop to think about why you dread an activity (such as exercising), it is probably because you consider it hard work. What if we could think about this in a different way? What if we considered it a joy instead of drudgery? How would that make you feel about going to the gym or taking that walk?

My challenge to you is to identify areas of your life that you deem "hard work." How can you make them more fun? How can they be transformed into joyous activities? If you sincerely give this the thought and consideration it deserves, I think you will find the answers. It is also possible that if you cannot come up with ways to transform them, these goals may not be as important to you as you previously thought. The act of pursuing goals and priorities in life should be joyous, since we are bombarded with so many things that actually have little to no impact on our quality of life. When we pursue those activities that we *consciously* have decided are significant to us, they truly should be thought of as "labors of love."

Lesson 7-- *Ask many questions.*

This may seem like a strange lesson to impart to people, but I'd like you to stop and think for a second about the most influential teachers in history-- Buddha, Jesus, Gandhi, etc. Despite their different religious and spiritual beliefs, what was one commonality among them as teachers and leaders? They all asked many questions. This is something I think we can do as well when we are leading others, but it's also something we can do by ourselves. In other words, we can ask *ourselves* probing questions--

"how," "why," "what," "where," etc. In my opinion, questions unlock the secrets of the universe. Remember the Biblical proverb, "Ask and you shall receive"? I firmly believe when you ask something of yourself with sincerity, you will find an answer. Your mind is trained to give you whatever you ask of it. Therefore, if this is the case, doesn't it make sense to ask only questions for which we want to receive answers? So be careful when you ask yourself negative questions like, "Why do these kinds of things always happen to me?" because your mind will search for an answer, like, "Because you're a dimwit!" However, if you ask uplifting, positive questions, such as, "How can I reach the next level of spiritual growth?" or "How can I increase the quality of the relationship I have with my significant other?" your mind will also search its inner recesses for answers to these questions as well. So be sure to ask only positive, uplifting questions and do away with the negative ones!

Here's an exercise I'd like you to try-- I call it the "Hundred Question" exercise because that's exactly what it is. I'd like you to grab a notepad and pen and find a quiet place to sit peacefully where you won't be disturbed for the duration of the exercise. Once you settle into a peaceful mindset, I would like you to let your mind go wild and start writing down questions about yourself, your life, your relationships, interests-- anything that is within your "sphere of control." Don't judge your questions at this point-- just keep that pen moving and get those questions written down.

Some examples might be, "How can I exercise every day?", "How can I increase my vitality and energy?" or "What does my perfect day look like?"

After you get these hundred questions written down, I'd like you go back and start looking for themes. In other words, are many of your questions about health, family, or how to start a business? Are most of them about how to appear more attractive to the opposite sex? These groupings of questions will give you a good idea of what your subconscious is deeming important. You might have three or four groupings of questions, maybe more or maybe less. Once you have some groupings, go back to examine each of them. These areas are what you want to focus on during your day. These are the areas your core being is telling you to focus on.

Now that you're used to asking questions, feel open to asking them in your day-to-day life. I think you'll be surprised at how much you learn about the world around you, what motivates people to do things, and how people see you in general. Also ask questions of *yourself*-- ask yourself things such as, "How can I become better at this?" or "How can I achieve my goals in this particular area of my life?" Because again, once you ask your brain a question, it will search all of its "memory banks" to deliver an answer to you, regardless of whether it is in fact accurate (or helpful). Therefore, obviously an important corollary to this is to ask *good questions*.

Lesson 8-- *Know that many times it's "two steps forward and one step back."*

This may seem like another apparent cliché that we all take for granted. Nevertheless, the thing about clichés is that many times there is a wealth of truth in them. Numerous times in my life, I have felt to be making progress on a project or with a business venture when something knocks me back, erasing weeks or months of work. If you think about it, though, even if you are moving "two steps forward, one step back," you are still moving forward! All it takes is the persistence to keep striving toward the objective or goal you set for yourself. Again, this requires you actually to *know* what your goals are-- what a concept!

Another proverb that I've heard many times in my life is, "It doesn't matter how many times you get knocked down, only how many times you get back up." Let's stop and think about that for a second. We all have setbacks in life-- challenges face us all. Many times, we will feel as if we have been "knocked down," or that life has treated us unfairly. The only thing that really matters, though, is whether we "get back up." In other words, do we, in spite of the pain, hurt feelings, or bruised ego, continue to move ourselves forward toward what we have our sights set on?

I'm a big believer in learning about the most successful people who have ever walked this earth. Since I was a little girl, I remember being fascinated about hearing stories of famous army generals, singers, and movie stars.

One thing they all had in common is that they were *not afraid to fail.* If you think about it, who's to say really what failure is? What if we simply thought differently about what failure means to us, or "re-labeled" what we previously thought as failure to something more positive, like a "learning experience"? There are many things that, looking back, I would have done differently in my personal life as well as my business life. If I think of those experiences and call them "failures," I begin to see those things, as well as much of my life in general, as a complete disappointment. However, if I "re-label" those things to "life experiences," or "learning experiences," those episodes suddenly seem a lot more bearable. I think to myself, "Yeah, I messed up, but everybody does when they're learning something." The other question I like to ask myself is "Well, what did I *learn* from that experience?" What a great point to ponder! If I can learn something from the experience, it's hasn't been a failure! I think we can all do this-- examine our day-to-day experiences, look at them in a new light, and our minds literally "reprocess" them to be, if not a completely positive experience, at least more neutral and much less debilitating.

Lesson 9-- *Recognize that you have to decide what success means to you individually.*

Although success is different for everybody, we can probably trace it to similar underlying feelings. If I were to ask you, "What does it mean to be successful?", I imagine that to begin you would give me an answer that is at least partly financially based. In other words, you'd tell me about the car, the house, the jewelry, etc. However, I would also imagine that as we began to delve deeper into what success is you would start to describe the *feelings* that you would have once you had become "successful." This would be feelings such as self-worth, self-esteem, security, etc. However, we have to have a clear picture in our minds of what the word *success* means to us. Does it mean retiring by age 50 and going to live in the Caribbean? Does it mean having the mountain cabin in Colorado? Does it mean having the security of knowing that you will never need to work another nine-to-five job? We need to get clear on what we're after-- how else would we know if we've arrived at our destination?

For me personally, success does include that material component, but there's also an element of self-worth involved. When I was a girl in Thailand, we had very little in the way of material possessions. We knew about the U.S., but what stood out to me, what I dreamed of becoming, was a movie star like the ones I had seen in the black-and-white movies that had come from America. I could sense the importance, the fan admiration, the high regard that was given to those starlets. That is what I wanted for myself. I enjoyed being in front of my classmates at school, solving problems on the board and reciting multiplication tables and the like. Their respect gave me the impulse to push forward with my learning. For me, then, a large part of *success* is gaining the approval of others, of being well respected, appreciated and admired.

Thus, the key question is, "What gets your inner fire burning the brightest?" What really motivates you to do your best every day? Here's something that I have done from time to time that I believe truly helps-- sit down with a pen and paper and just start writing about what is important to you. What are your goals for the next year, five years, ten years, thirty years? Just let your mind get creative-- do not put any limits on what is "possible" or not. Just let your pen get things on paper. Do you want that beach condominium in Florida? Put it down. Do you want that luxury vehicle in the next year? Put it down. Just allow your mind to move freely. Realize everybody's definition of success is different and that many times we don't even actually have a clear idea of what our *own* definition is!

After you do this, go back and begin to put timelines on these items. By when do you want to have the luxury car? One year, three years, five years? Get the timelines down. Now things should start to feel more tangible. Remember the old acronym SMART (Specific, Measurable, Attainable, Realistic, and Trackable) as it relates to goal setting? In case you're not familiar with this acronym, let me elaborate a little bit on this, since it describes the essence of how our goals should be. For a goal to be *specific* means that we should try to quantify (put numbers to) our goals when at all possible. For example, have you or someone you know ever set some sort of weight-loss goal to the extent of, "I want to lose weight"? What's wrong with this goal? Granted, an imprecise goal is better than no goal at all, but the goal can be made much better (and therefore more likely to be attained) if it is quantified or made more specific. For example, it could be modified to something such as, "I want to lose 15 pounds by May 1." Now that really makes things clear for your mind to pursue and leaves no room for doubt.

Secondly, and this goes along with the first one, a goal needs to be *measurable.* In other words, it needs to be designed in such a way that you can tell with very little analysis if you are getting closer to your goal or further away. In other words, design your goals in terms of pounds, dollars, weeks, months, or any other tangible, quantifiable terms. Of course, with health and financial goals this is inherently quite easy. We have been trained to think in terms of pounds or dollars. However, this could also be used when setting other goals, such as lowering your blood pressure or cholesterol levels. Blood pressure is measured in terms of two numbers, the systolic and diastolic pressures. We can measure these two numbers very easily by taking our blood pressure. For cholesterol levels, there are two numbers to represent the good and bad types of cholesterol. We can measure these with a blood test when we get a medical check-up. Other things that can be lowered through careful monitoring are things like blood sugar, triglyceride levels, etc. If it is a financial goal, obviously the first thing that comes to mind is dollars (more specifically, how many dollars do we want?). However, other things such as net worth (assets minus liabilities) are also beneficial when looking at financial goals that are easily measurable. For any goal, we must be able to know through measurable, quantifiable terms if we are approaching our goal or getting further away.

The third and fourth parts of the SMART acronym are for a goal to be *attainable* and *realistic.* In my view, there is a fine line between being attainable and/or realistic and being overly aggressive with your goal setting. I am always hesitant to tell someone that his or her goal is not realistic or attainable. I mean, who am I to tell someone something like this? I believe it is essentially up to us to answer that question of whether something is realistic. However, clearly some goals are more or less realistic than others are. For example, if I tell someone that I want to lose 15 pounds by tomorrow, there is clearly no physical way for me to attain something like this-- it is not a realistic goal. However, if you tell me that your goal is to be a millionaire by next year, and you have a viable plan on how to achieve this aspiration, who am I to tell you that this is not attainable? In my view, goal setting is an extremely personal type of activity. However, this is not to say that we can't share our goals with others-- sometimes it gives you an extra impetus to feel that you are accountable to other people with regard to your goals. Again, I believe that each person must look deep down and determine if a goal is realistic and attainable. If it is too aggressive, you run the risk of becoming disillusioned with the goal setting process and never set another goal in this area. If you shoot too low, you run the risk of not setting your sights high enough. There is a fine line between the two ends of the spectrum.

The last part of the acronym is *trackable*. In other words, we need to be able to track our progress over time. Combined with the first two parts, *specific* and *measurable*, this should be very straightforward. In other words, we should be able to track our proximity to the goal on a daily, weekly or monthly basis. Of course, you should always write your initial goal down, and I recommend tracking your goal over time in the same place-- I suggest a notebook of some sort. For example, suppose that your initial goal was to lose 10 pounds within a two-month period. You could then also track your progress over the weeks by weighing in every Sunday morning, for example, and writing those figures down as well. By glancing at these figures over the weeks, you could then determine very quickly if you are approaching your goal or falling farther away from it.

Does this mean that you will always achieve every goal that you set for yourself? No, of course not. However, using these sorts of strategies will drastically improve your odds of reaching your goals, especially if you also develop a plan toward the goal's attainment along with reasons why you need to achieve the goal and what you will miss if you do not achieve it.

Use all these tips to make your goals as real to you as possible. Again, I would suggest that you go sit down in a quiet place, try to enter into a creative state of mind, pull out that pen and notebook, and begin writing. Don't let your mind restrict itself either; in other words, don't let your mind tell you, "Oh, you'll never achieve that." Just let those thoughts flow freely. After you have your list, go back and pick out the most important goals to you-- maybe the top three or four. They could be anything on your list-- simply try to determine what you value the most. Then I'd like you to get clear on *why* you want those things. It's funny, and really somewhat mystical, but our minds are extremely powerful when it knows *what* it wants and *why* it wants it. So get clear on your rationale for why you want those top three or four things. Write at least a paragraph or two. Be sure that you are as specific as possible. Your mind does well with detail and precision. In other words, why exactly do you want that mountain cabin? If your rationale is to have a secret getaway for yourself and your special someone, describe in detail the feelings you'll get, the experiences you'll help create, and the memories that you'll forge from that particular possession.

The next tip that I would tell you as far as *how* to achieve the goals you set for yourself is to try to *take action* as soon as possible-- do something that will help you to achieve your goals. In other words, if you want to write that novel, immediately go sit down in front of the computer and get an outline done, get the title page done, write the first page, etc. If you want that sports car, research it on the internet, look in an auto magazine to see what the current prices are, call a dealership to see what models they have in stock, etc. The idea is to develop momentum to launch you forward. We can have the best goals in the world, with clear rationales as to why we want them, and great ways to measure progress, but if we don't take action, the rest is for naught. *So do something.* Several years ago when I was considering a business to open, I spent hours researching on the internet and reading the business magazines. I didn't know exactly the type of business that I wanted, but I knew that being self-employed was the only way to go. Thus, I was ready to take as much action as necessary to build up the momentum I needed to propel me forward.

Again, everybody's definition of success is different. Take some time to determine what yours is. Otherwise, when you achieve whatever it is you thought you desired, it's quite possible that you look up and wonder, "*Why* was it that I wanted this?" On the other hand, if you're clear on what you want, why you want it, and have a viable plan for how to attain it, the universe will find a way to provide it to you.

Lesson 10-- *Take care of your holistic self.*

When we're really motoring toward our goals, it's quite easy to neglect parts of our physical, mental, and spiritual selves. For even the most seemingly successful individuals, who have risen to the zenith of their professional careers, if they are not healthy (physically, mentally and spiritually), what do they truly have? I'm sure you know someone who has been extraordinarily successful only to die of a sudden heart attack at a relatively young age. I've personally known many people like this over the years and have read and heard about many others like them. One of the things that strikes me is the thought that at first glance it seemed like they had everything, but in many cases, they didn't take care of themselves nearly as well as they should have. In other words, they struggled nearly all of their lives to get to where they wanted to be professionally, and were beginning to enjoy the fruits of their labor, only to be taken early and thus unable to enjoy the harvest. Now granted, sometimes people do everything in their power to take care of themselves on all levels and still succumb to disease much too young, but for the most part, it's those who don't give their bodies the respect they deserve that are not able to enjoy into ripe old age the many blessings of a life fulfilled.

I'm a firm believer in the adage, "Our health is our greatest wealth." If we are healthy in all aspects of our being, there is nothing we cannot accomplish if we put our minds to it and have an organized plan and strategy for achieving it. However, if we are not healthy, it makes it extremely difficult to achieve anything. In other words, our health is the foundation upon which all our other life goals and objectives are built. Again, when I refer to health, I'm referring to the term in its most holistic, broadest sense-- mental, spiritual, and physical health. It's not enough to be physically healthy if we suffer from anxiety, depression, constant loneliness, or spiritual emptiness. We need to recognize that our bodies, minds, and souls each have unique needs, and do our best to fulfill those needs.

I must confess that I didn't always think like this nor am I perfect in this regard. Earlier in my adult life I smoked occasionally-- especially in social situations-- and have always enjoyed alcoholic beverages. Many times I still let stress get the better of me. However, as I've gotten older, I've realized the effects of these things truly do accumulate over time. I think what makes people discount the effects of these negative actions on one's well-being is the fact that the effects are so slow to manifest themselves. For example, it literally takes years for the effects of regular smoking or drinking to be visibly apparent.

Have you ever looked at pictures of yourself from five or ten years before and thought, "Gosh, I look young there" or what's worse, "Gosh, I look so much *older* now"? Why is that? Well, obviously I'm not a doctor and only have what I've read in books and on the internet to back me up, but apparently the body contains something called *free-radicals* that are the primary culprits behind heart disease, cancer and almost all other effects of what we consider old age. Although some of these free radicals are produced as a natural result of living our daily lives (through the oxidative process in the body), when we drink, smoke, or experience stress, our body produces more of these free radicals. They wreak havoc in our bodies because they lack a "partner" and want to attach to other paired-up cells, thereby destroying healthy cells in order to attain this molecular stability. Fortunately, there are ways to combat this destructive process-- through ingesting vitamins and foods that contain *antioxidants*. These nutrients actually neutralize the free radicals so that they are no longer a threat. Some common antioxidants are such nutrients as Vitamins C, E and A (which are found in many fruits and vegetables) as well as other things like Zinc, Selenium and Omega-3 fatty acids (such as those found in fish).

Although many doctors now recommend these types of nutrients in the form of supplements-- however, consult with your own physician to see if these types of supplements are right for you-- there are other things that we can do to help minimize the production of free radicals. These are such things as proper nutrition, stress reduction, adequate sleep, moderate exercise, laughter, and a positive outlook on life. This is where the science of body and mind begin to overlap.

Lesson 11-- *Don't "should" all over yourself.*

It's very easy to go through life looking back on what you "should've done." I have been guilty of this more times than I'd care to admit and despite my best intentions, still occasionally catch myself doing it. Have you ever heard the expression that "hindsight is 20/20"? What exactly does this mean? To me it means that when we look back on a choice or decision we had in the past, it's very easy to second-guess ourselves and think, "But the choice now seems so clear. Why didn't I go that route to begin with?" Of course, when we make a decision, we do so with what is called *imperfect information.* We never have *every single piece* of information we could have in order to make the best decision-- we do so with the most complete information we have at the time.

So in fact we could play the "should've" game with ourselves with just about every decision we ever make in life, because it's only once the decision is made and the results and consequences of that decision begin to manifest themselves do we truly see the impact of the initial decision. In my view, the major problem with this "should've" type of mentality is that if we allow it to spin out of control, it can dominate all of our decision-making, and thus our whole lives. We begin to feel "gun shy," a state of mental paralysis in which we are hesitant to make any type of decision for fear of making the wrong one.

I believe we all have a "decision-making muscle." I consider this in the same way as I would a physical muscle. It must be toned, exercised, and taken care of in order to grow, stay strong, and serve us when we need it. We should attempt to "flex" our decision-making muscle whenever we can by making decisions without fearing potential mistakes or regrets. This is not to say that we should not try to get all the information possible before we make a decision, especially one with more important consequences. Again, we will never have all possible information, so at some point we have to "pull the trigger" and make the best possible decision *given the information we possess at that point in time.* In other words, don't be afraid of mistakes. We will always make mistakes because we are human and that's our nature. The key, of course, as I imagine you've heard many times in different contexts, is to learn from them.

Over the years, I've spoken in-depth with and read biographies of many elderly people, some of whom achieved great things over the course of their lives. There seems to be a common theme when it comes to not "shoulding." In general, it seems when looking back upon their lives, they don't tend to regret things they did-- they regret the things they *didn't do.* When you stop for a second to think about this, it's really a powerful idea. Many times in our own daily lives, we look at something and think, "No, I shouldn't try that," or "No, I shouldn't approach this person." However, most folks who have lived their "three score and ten" (or beyond) on this earth, when looking back on life and pondering their existence, do not think that way. Most look back and think things like, "I wish I had started that business like I wanted to," or "I wish I had approached that person I was so attracted to." My challenge to both you and myself is to go ahead and attempt what it is you want-- go ahead and risk being "rejected" or experiencing temporary "failure." We will ultimately be so much more satisfied with our lives if we try and do not succeed than not to have tried at all.

Lesson 12-- *When you fall, be willing to get back up, brush yourself off, and be ready for more.*

Life is all about risk, about taking chances, and about "failing" many times before you actually reach your goals. I put the word "failing" in quotation marks because what we consider failure many times could be thought of as simply a learning experience on our way to achieving our objective. Have you ever heard the saying, "Nothing worth doing is easy"? To me this means if a goal is worthy of attainment-- for example, the new sports car, the successful business, or learning to play a musical instrument-- it will require time, energy, and focus. I've always been one to look at life as being like a game-- in some cases you win and in some you lose. However, again, as has been a constant theme throughout this book, you only fail when you *stop trying*. It goes back to the idea of persistence-- as the great football coach Vince Lombardi put it, "Never, never, never, never, ever quit." This was great advice from one of the most successful coaches in NFL history. This sentiment was also echoed by Winston Churchill during the darkest days of World War II, when Allied victory was far from certain. Many historians give him credit for greatly lifting the morale of not only England, but of the United States and other Allied countries.

Many times in life we tend to imagine the worst possible outcome for any given situation and focus on that exclusively. That could mean starting a business and going broke as a result, being hired for a new job and it exposing your lack of knowledge or approaching a special person and being rejected. However, most times the worst outcome does not happen. There's a saying that "Bad luck is fickle," meaning that it would be equally or more likely to have a positive outcome occur. Nevertheless, many times this imaginary fear can paralyze us into not doing anything at all-- being afraid to try. We as humans tend to build things up in our minds, and as I have heard many times in psychology circles, our brains will do more to *avoid pain* than to *acquire pleasure*. Although we may want to undertake that business venture, our minds tend to tell us, "If I start a business there's a good chance I'll lose all I have", or "I'd like to approach that person that I'm attracted to, but if I do, I'll probably end up getting hurt." That's true, but if you never try, you'll never know and will always wonder.

The Roman philosopher Seneca, writing to his friend Lucilius, put it very inspiringly: "This is the touchstone of such a spirit; no prizefighter can go with high spirits into the strife if he has never been beaten black and blue; the only contestant who can confidently enter the lists is the man who has seen his own blood, who has felt his teeth rattle beneath his opponent's fist, who has been tripped and felt the full force of his adversary's charge, who has been downed in body but not in spirit, one who, as often as he falls, rises again with greater defiance than ever" (Letter 13). These words, no matter how many times I read them, never cease to move my spirit. In my mind, this is declaring that life's challenges should not be avoided, but embraced. Once we earn the "bruises" that many times life imparts upon us, once we have "seen our own blood," we are emboldened-- fear literally has no power over us any more.

Much of this is related to mindset and the label you put on the experience we tend to call "failure." For most people, failure means pain. They visualize failure in their minds and feel a gut-level reaction to it. They will many times end up not attempting the thing they were considering because of the potential pain they think they would experience if they didn't achieve the desired outcome. What if we were to rename the experience formerly known as "failure" to something else, such as "learning"? So even if we didn't achieve the desired outcome the first time around, at least we learned something-- we made further distinctions to help us in the future attainment of the outcome. There's a well know story about Thomas Edison prior to his invention of the light bulb. Someone at one point asked him if he felt like a failure since he had "failed" in so many experiments to refine the light bulb. His simple reply was that, "I have not failed; I've simply discovered 999 ways how not to create the light bulb." Therein lies a golden nugget of wisdom that we can all use. It is very easy for us not to achieve our desired outcome the first couple of times around, give up, and consider that we "failed." It is also just as easy, after not achieving the desired outcome the first couple of times around, to continue forward after having "learned."

Teddy Roosevelt gave a famous speech in Paris that also has inspired generations. "It is not the critic who counts: not the man who points out how the strong man stumbles or where the doer of deeds could have done better. The credit belongs to the man who is actually in the arena, whose face is marred by dust and sweat and blood, who strives valiantly, who errs and comes up short again and again, because there is no effort without error or shortcoming, but who knows the great enthusiasms, the great devotions, who spends himself for a worthy cause; who, at the best, knows, in the end, the triumph of high achievement, and who, at the worst, if he fails, at least he fails while daring greatly, so that his place shall never be with those cold and timid souls who knew neither victory nor defeat" (Roosevelt, 1910). The choice is ours-- do we merely "exist" through life or do we truly have the courage to live?

Lesson 13-- *Be grateful.*

This is such an important lesson because we can achieve all of our goals and seem very successful to others around us, but if we don't feel grateful, we will not *feel* as though we accomplished what it is we wanted. To feel grateful, to feel blessed for what we have, is something that almost all religions preach as one of their major tenets.

Doesn't it seem strange that most all religions over the course of time, including modern ones, preach a similar precept? Shouldn't that tell us something? In my view, this is the key to having a rich (in all senses of the word, not just financial), happy life-- to be grateful, to give thanks to a higher power, and to feel blessed for all we have been given. I think you will find that if you do this on a regular basis, it will enrichen your life in ways you cannot imagine. It can also radically change your state of mind whenever you happen to feel down-- just focus on that for which you are grateful.

Also, remember nothing is intrinsically good or bad-- it's how we interpret the events that happen to us that have the power to give them meaning. There's an old Buddhist story that goes something like this. An old farmer and his son lived in an abandoned shack on the side of a hill. Their only possession of value was a horse. One day the horse ran away. The neighbors came by to offer sympathy. "That's terrible!" they said. "We'll see," replied the old farmer. The next day the horse returned, bringing with it several wild horses. The old man shut them all inside the gate. The neighbors hurried over. "That's wonderful!" they said. "We'll see," replied the farmer. The following day, the son tried riding one of the wild horses, fell off, and broke his leg. The neighbors came around as soon as they heard the news. "How tragic!" they said. "We'll see," replied the old farmer. The day after that, the army came through, forcing the local young men to fight a faraway battle against the northern barbarians. Many of them would never return. However, the son could not go, because he had broken his leg.

Do you see the moral of this traditional tale? Nothing that happens to us is inherently good or bad-- it is the meaning we attach that makes it so. Thus, be grateful not only for the good fortune you experience on a daily basis-- give thanks for life's challenges as well, because these are the events that actually make us grow in mind and spirit. Granted, no rational person seeks out tragedy or misfortune, but they are an inevitable part of life. Of course, we can easily embrace life's wonderful experiences, but we also must be mature enough in spirit to accept the difficulties that life inevitably brings and seek to grow from them.

Again, take out your notebook and let's get to work. I'd like you to begin writing down all the major areas of your life-- personal, professional, civic, etc. Then I'd like you to begin describing things you're grateful for under each of these major areas. Under "Personal," you may even want to break this down into "Friendship," "Health" or other subcategories that make sense to you. Spend some time with yourself digging into what you feel grateful for, what makes you feel blessed, what makes you feel as if you have truly been given a gift by God or a Higher Power. Try to delve as deeply as you can into *why* this makes you feel that way.

Now that you've finished this, go back and read these things. How do they make you feel about being alive and your mission on this earth? If reading these things does not inspire you, perhaps you have not done a good enough job of describing for what it is you are grateful. Feel free to read this back to yourself on a daily basis, or whenever you feel you need a dose of inspiration.

Lesson 14-- *Feed your mind.*

The mind is like any other organ in the body-- it must be fed and cared for. To me, the best way to feed your mind is to read, study and take in inspirational words of wisdom from those who have come before us. In fact, it is so important that I have dedicated an entire later chapter to it. I ask that you commit to reading at least 30 minutes a day of uplifting, inspiring literature-- something that will broaden your horizons, inspire you with ideas, and stimulate you to reach for the next step in your life. If you do this consistently over time, you will find that your life completely changes as a result.

Chapter VII
Top Ten Tips for Optimum Health

If we have our physical health, it's so much easier to accomplish all the other things that we want to do in our lives. On the other hand, we can be full of ambition, yet if we do not have the physical energy to tackle our projects, our ambition is for naught. Although we tend to take our health for granted, our health is certainly not guaranteed-- it is something that we must work at every day to maintain. With that said, here are my "Top Ten" tips for maintaining life-long health.

1. *Walk about 30 minutes a day, every day.* This can be done outside, weather permitting, or inside on a treadmill. Although outdoors is actually healthier, because our bodies require a certain amount of sunshine and the Vitamin D that sunshine provides, walking on a treadmill is fine when weather doesn't allow otherwise.

Walking is one of the few exercise activities we can do every day of our lives because it is relatively low impact. However, if you walk fast enough (at least about 3.5 miles per hour), it can also serve as a wonderful form of cardiovascular exercise and even helps to improve muscle tone. If you look online these days, you will find a plethora of information regarding walking and the health benefits that it affords. In fact, if you examine the most long-lived cultures around the world-- in some parts of Italy, Ecuador, and France, for example-- a key component of their daily rituals is walking. Although not necessarily in the form of recreational exercise, it is something that is part of their daily routines, like walking to the market, walking to visit a neighbor, walking to and from work, etc.

If you do not feel like you can get in 30 minutes at once, try breaking up your walk into different segments-- three short walks of ten minutes each, for example. The studies that I have read indicate that the benefits of breaking up your walking time are equivalent to those of a longer walk. Besides the pure cardiovascular and muscle-toning benefits, in my opinion it's also a great therapeutic type activity. Many times I go for a walk simply when I have something on my mind. I can mull it over, kick around different ideas, and many times come up with a solution during the walk itself or shortly thereafter-- just be sure to keep a notebook nearby to jot down any thoughts that come to mind. So if you are looking for an exercise you can do anywhere, under almost any circumstances, with minimal equipment (just a good pair of walking shoes) and already are an expert in, consider walking.

2. *Eat sparingly.* Although this could incorporate several ideas, what I am specifically referring to is to eat slightly less than what your body requires. Studies have shown that people who eat slightly less that what their bodies need, and never stuff themselves during a meal, live longer lives. A

corollary to this idea is not to eat large quantities later in the day, after about 4 PM-- eat your biggest meals for breakfast and lunch. If nothing else, this will help you to maintain your bodyweight and probably sleep better as well. An easy way to reduce calories quickly is to cut back on junk food, sweets and soda.

3. *Get plenty of sleep.* Research has shown that humans perform best with about eight hours of sleep, although this can vary slightly from person to person. If you can't get a full eight hours during the night, for whatever reason, don't be afraid to take a nap during the early afternoon if possible. Sleep is truly a magical thing-- it's when our bodies restore and heal themselves. Many cultures and civilizations over the centuries have revered sleep as a cure-all and a gift from the gods. I would have to agree. If you're anything like me, you know how awful you feel after a poor night's sleep and how wonderful you feel after a pleasant, restful night's sleep. Beyond the restorative properties of sleep, it's also a marvelous way that we as humans can solve problems, let our minds form new relationships between complex thoughts and ideas, and sort through the challenges of the day gone by and prepare for the challenges of the day to come. Don't feel guilty about needing your sleep-- your body will reward you for it ten-fold.

4. *Establish friendships and work on keeping them.* Human beings are social creatures. We all have an innate need to be with others, exchange ideas, share thoughts, and feel

connections with those around us. It is truly rare to find someone who has no desire to be with others to some degree or another. Although intuitively we know this and possess a strong urge to socialize and be with others from a young age, scientific studies have been able to prove over the last few years that we will live longer, healthier lives the more we socialize.

Although we usually have no problem making friends when we are children and through our teen and early adult years, as time passes we normally find it harder to make new friends. I'm not exactly sure why this is, but I would think it has something to do with the simple fact that most adults are much *too busy* to make new friends. So much of our lives at that point revolves around work and family that we have little time or energy to actively seek out new friendships. That's where churches, social organizations and the like come in. They allow us as adults to have the opportunity to be around like-minded people and create acquaintances and friendships. It's extremely important for us to create and maintain friendships-- the latter of which is much harder than the former, in my opinion. We will live longer, happier lives and be able to add texture to our lives they otherwise might not have.

5. *Exercise your mind every day.* The mind is like the body in the sense that it needs to be exercised, cared for, "stretched," and not allowed to atrophy. I mentioned the importance of walking every day for a half-hour. I believe it

is also important to exercise your mind in some capacity for at least a half-hour a day as well. This "mental exercise" can be in myriad forms-- reading something uplifting, studying a language, doing crossword puzzles or other mental brainteasers, reading a publication of interest to you, etc. The type of exercise is not as important as the act of doing *something* every day to stimulate your mind.

The mind is very similar to any other muscle in the body in the sense that it can grow stronger with exercise, or it can atrophy from lack of exercise. Let me ask you something-- have you ever gone for a period without really challenging yourself mentally and then suddenly realizing you do not seem as "sharp" as you perhaps once were? Alternatively, have you ever gone for a period of time in which you were reading every day, studying something, playing chess, doing word puzzles, etc. for a consistent period and then suddenly realized you seemed very "sharp" indeed? That's the power of exercising your mind. It grows stronger and weakens just like any other muscle in your body. However, there is one big difference-- your mind is perhaps the most important muscle of the body because it controls all else that we do, mentally, spiritually and physically. We can have a healthy mind and unhealthy body and still live some semblance of a normal life, but not with an unhealthy mind (i.e. Alzheimer's disease, stroke, or countless other diseases that affect mental well-being) and healthy body. So treat your brain as well-- if not better-- than you treat you body.

6. *Laugh as much as possible.* The act of laughing, besides being one of the great pleasurable experiences of life, is extremely healthy for you. Studies have shown it releases endorphins, or pleasure chemicals, into your body, which produce a sense of well-being. It also helps to strengthen the immune system and can actually make you feel younger. I've read stories about people who were suffering from illnesses that, as part of their own self-treatment regimen, watched funny movies and shows in order literally to laugh as much as possible.

The most famous story of "laughter as medicine" is that of Norman Cousins. Cousins was the editor of *The Saturday Review* for over 30 years, and wrote numerous books including *Anatomy of an Illness*. In 1964, he returned home from a meeting in Moscow experiencing severe joint pain and with a high fever. He was diagnosed with a collagen illness that attacks the connective tissues of the body. Cousins had read of how negative emotions can be harmful to the body, and so hypothesized if negative emotions were detrimental to one's health, then positive emotions should improve health. He was initially treated with high doses of painkillers, which he realized were harmful to his body. This motivated him to self-prescribe a medication of a different sort. He hired a nurse who would read humorous stories and play Marx Brothers movies for him. This proved to be effective, and in very little time Cousins was off all the painkillers and sleeping pills. He found that the laughter relieved pain and would help him sleep. He published his story and claims of the benefits of laughter. However, he was received with a great deal of criticism at that time. Fortunately, modern medical science has come to acknowledge the physiological benefits of laughter. Norman Cousins declared that he "laughed himself out of" a deadly disease and scientists have since that time come to theorize that laughter has the ability to strengthen the human immune system (Cousins, 1979).

Here's another great perspective on laughter, by the great nineteenth century American writer Mark Twain. Twain very aptly stated that, "The human race has only one really effective weapon, and that's laughter. The moment it arises, all our hardnesses yield, all our irritations and resentments slip away, and a sunny spirit takes their place." (www.thinkexist.com/quotation). If that's not motivation enough to laugh as much as possible every day, I don't know what is.

7. *Eat as many fruits and vegetables as you can.* This is something you read about a great deal these days, but it is worth mentioning here because it is so crucial to long-term health. One of the great things about fruits and vegetables is the antioxidants that they possess, which have the power to prevent heart disease and cancer, the top two leading causes of death in both males and females in this country. They also

are low in calories, full of vitamins and minerals that our bodies need for their natural functioning, and full of fiber for the healthy functioning of our digestive system. For those of us who have a sweet tooth, fruit is a natural alternative to refined desserts such as cookies, cake, and ice cream.

According to medical studies, we should eat at least five servings of fruits and vegetables per day. I personally find that I can get at least three of those servings in my morning smoothie, which I prepare with a base of low calorie juice, a banana, assorted frozen fruits (my favorites are blueberries, blackberries and strawberries), some low-fat yogurt and then a sprinkle of flaxseed, which is also very heart-healthy. I have done this now for about the last five years at least four or five times a week (the other days I might have some scrambled eggs or high-fiber cereal). I've seen all types of expensive juicing machines on the market, but I use a simple blender to create my smoothies. If you try smoothies and find that you enjoy them, don't be afraid to experiment with different fruits and other ingredients-- there really is no *wrong* way to make a delicious smoothie. If you find that you don't enjoy them, please take the time to find other ways to sneak at least five servings of fruits and vegetables into your daily diet. Your body will truly thank you for it.

8. *Have a hobby.* I believe that having a hobby we truly enjoy and immerse ourselves in is tremendously beneficial to our mental and spiritual well-being. Although our interests and

hobbies obviously change over the years-- I know mine certainly have-- I have found that this is a natural process as we *evolve* as human beings. My hobbies over the years have ranged from working with flower arrangements to photography. I think the key to a good hobby is that it should be something that engages you fully and you would do even if you thought you would never make any money from it. Ideally, a hobby could evolve into something that would represent a profitable venture for you, as my hobby with jewelry eventually grew into my jewelry store. However, obviously many times when you initially become interested in a hobby you are not sure if you could ever make any money from it. Again, I think many times a new hobby just occurs naturally and that it should be something we embrace and always are on the lookout for.

If you currently do not have any hobbies but would like to have one, you can ask yourself questions such as, "What interests me?" and, "What kind of work would I do for free?" Those kinds of questions can many times help you to identify in what areas you are interested. Regardless of what your hobbies are, I would encourage you to spend as much time as is reasonably possible (given your circumstances) with your hobby because it can stimulate you in many aspects of your well-being and one never knows where a hobby will lead. Many celebrities over the years, such as singers and actors, started their craft as simple hobbies. Dare to dream big, but also be willing to spend time with your hobby simply for the sheer enjoyment.

9. *Drink plenty of water.* Drinking an adequate amount of water is one of the easiest, but most overlooked, aspects of achieving and maintaining good health. I have read many times over the last few years that our bodies need at least eight full glasses of water each day to maintain the proper functioning of the body. I know that my own body needs at least this, if not more, since I am quite active (I am still at my store almost every day for at least eight hours a day, most of which is spent on my feet). The thing about our bodies, however, is that once we actually *feel* dehydrated, our body is actually much overdue for liquid. I keep bottled water in the mini-refrigerator at the store since I don't have access to tap water there.

Speaking of tap water, I know that the trend over the last 10 to 15 years has been for people to move away from it in favor of bottled water of all sorts, much of which is quite expensive. However, the most recent studies I've come across have indicated that most tap water in the U.S. is as safe as bottled water, if not more so. Another benefit of tap water is that it contains a good deal of fluoride, which helps to protect our teeth-- something which bottled water apparently does not have. I would say unless you absolutely don't have access to tap water, or are traveling in a foreign country where you are just not sure about the quality of the tap water, don't feel compelled to drink only bottled water.

Regardless of your source of water, however, be sure always to get enough of it. I'm sure you've heard that our bodies are about two-thirds water. This to me is evidence enough that we need to provide our bodies with enough to keep that balance and maintain in proper state all the physiological functions of the body of which water is a part.

10. *If you drink, do so moderately-- but never smoke.* I've always liked alcoholic beverages. That may come as a surprise to you, but it's true. In fact, at times during the course of my adult life, I've battled with drinking too much. To me, a drink-- a bottle of beer or a glass of wine-- has always been a way to relax and a reward for a long day's work. In fact, I still drink from time to time, but I feel that as I get older, I really can't drink as much as I did when I was younger and still feel rested and strong the next day. However, for those of us who like to drink, we can take heart in the fact that most scientific studies have shown that moderate alcohol consumption-- about one drink a day-- is actually healthy. In fact, studies have indicated that it helps to protect against heart disease and other leading causes of death. Again, the key is just not to abuse it.

Smoking, on the other hand, has absolutely no redeeming health properties. In fact, it's quite the opposite. Smoking, as I'm sure you're aware, leads to a variety of diseases and illnesses, not to mention yellow teeth and bad breath ("smoker's breath"). Although I smoked a little when I was in my early 20s, I never really developed a taste for it.

I'm fortunate that this was the case, however, because smoking is highly addictive-- ask anyone that's ever tried to quit. So whatever you do, please do not get into the habit of smoking. There is nothing "cool" about it and has no positive merits. If you're already a smoker, please do whatever you need to do to quit. It has been proven that the human body can actually heal itself from the detrimental effects of smoking within a relatively short period. The lungs and other organs affected by smoking start to regenerate after only a few days of not smoking. That's positive news indeed.

Chapter VIII
Thoughts for Reflection

One of the previous lessons referenced the notion that we should all commit to reading something uplifting for 30 minutes a day. I know this sounds tough, and it probably will be at first, but it is essential in our growth as human beings. I would like to share some thoughts with you now that I ask you to contemplate. These are the kinds of things we can pick up from our daily readings-- ideas, words of wisdom, and insights from the best and most influential minds in history.

1. **"The journey of a thousand miles must begin with a single step." - Lao Tzu**

I have heard this thought in one form or another almost all of my life. I believe to heed these words would serve us well because when faced with a big project, many times we feel daunted by its sheer size-- something that can prevent us from even attempting the project. As I've reiterated throughout this text, I'm a bit of a dreamer and like to think big. Psychologically, how do I gear myself up to tackle a large, seemingly endless project? I try to tell myself all I need to do is to get started, take that first step, and everything else will fall into place.

When doing the research for this book, I came across an interesting concept called "Don't Break the Chain." It is based on Jerry Seinfeld's personal system of getting into the writing habit. When he was actively writing for the Seinfeld show, he would hang a big yearly calendar on the wall. For every day he sat down to write, he would make a large red "X" over it on the calendar. According to him, "After a few days you'll have a chain. Just keep at it and the chain will grow longer every day. You'll like seeing that chain, especially when you get a few weeks under your belt. Your only job next is to not break the chain" (Mears, 2011). Although this is a wonderfully simple idea, it is remarkably effective-- but then again, some of the best ideas are indeed the simplest. What is the lesson behind this? To me, it's that every project, even the largest ones, can be broken down into small, manageable steps. Seinfeld certainly understood the power of this idea, as his show Seinfeld went on for nine seasons and was one of the most successful sitcoms in all of television history. Thus, whatever the project is, just take the first step. You will be amazed at how the first step will lead to the second, the second to the third, and so on until one day you realize you have completed the once overwhelming project.

2. **"There are no limits. There are plateaus, but you must not stay there, you must go beyond them. If it kills you, it kills you. A man must constantly exceed his level." - Bruce Lee**

This is a very inspiring quote from a man who truly lived his passion. This idea of breaking through plateaus motivates me to a great degree because we all experience them, even the greatest athletes, scientists, leaders, and movie stars of all time. When I read things like this, I feel these types of people were indeed human also, and that I should not despair when I feel stuck from time to time. There's no shame in feeling you are on a plateau of sorts in your life, whether professionally, with your important relationships, or with anything else of value to you. However, what *is* a shame is to allow yourself to be stagnant and not reach beyond where you happen to be now. A corollary to this idea is the old adage of, "Never rest on your laurels." In other words, don't allow yourself to feel so satisfied with your accomplishments that you fail to reach for the next level of achievement. It's perfectly acceptable to be proud of what you've done and of things you've accomplished. However, don't let that impede you from continually reaching forward.

3. "I have come to understand that life is best to be lived and not to be conceptualized. I am happy because I am growing daily and I honestly do not know where the limit lies. To be certain, every day there can be a revelation or a new discovery. I treasure the memory of the past misfortunes. It has added more to my bank of fortitude." - Bruce Lee

This is another quote from the great martial artist. This quote encapsulates the risk that living life inherently is. Life is dangerous, and perhaps that is the way it is supposed to be. While this idea is worth noting in and of itself, the above quote also captures the idea that personal growth is one of the most worthwhile goals we as individuals can pursue. I've heard it said we are only happy when we are growing as individuals and contributing to others. I believe there is a great deal of truth in this. Have you ever felt stagnant in your life? I know I have. How did that make you feel? If you're anything like me, it probably made you feel somewhat depressed and with a soured outlook on life. What does Mr. Lee tell us in the above quote? He's happy because he's growing daily. We can all grow daily in many facets of our lives, but we have to make a conscious decision that we *choose* to grow daily. There are many distractions in our lives and many other things that compete for our attention on a daily basis. Thus, we consciously have to decide what is most important to us and what we want to focus on in terms of personal and/or professional growth. Inherent in this idea is the concept of prioritizing our lives-- deciding where we desire to focus our mental, spiritual, and physical energy.

While sometimes finding the time to actually do those things we consider important can seem like a daunting task, psychologists and others in the field of human performance affirm if we can simply improve by a mere one percent a day, over time this seemingly small effort will yield very noteworthy results. For example, if we decide that learning to play the guitar is a priority for us, focus our attention on this, and vow to improve by this amount per day, over time we will be immeasurably ahead of where we were months, or even weeks, before. Now granted, this doesn't seem like a lot, but over time, it compounds and truly adds up. One of my challenges to you is to identify those things that are in fact important to you and try to improve just *one percent* a day.

The other part of this quote is the part at the end regarding misfortune. In Western culture, we are taught to try to avoid risk to minimize possible misfortune. Here is a radical idea though. What if we learn to embrace misfortune because with misfortune comes internal fortitude, inner strength, and mental and spiritual toughness? I am not saying that we should like misfortune or seek it out in any way. However, what I *am* saying is that we should recognize that misfortune is a part of life-- that it's inevitable and we should not beat ourselves up over it or necessarily even dread it. Have you ever heard the adage, "What doesn't kill us makes us stronger"? Although this is sometimes overused in our culture to the point of almost being a cliché, there is a wealth of truth in this. Remind yourself that misfortune is a natural "byproduct" of life, and we all have challenges to overcome. How we view these challenges and misfortunes is what makes all the difference.

4. "We are what we repeatedly do. Excellence then, is not an act, but a habit." - Aristotle

It is an inspiring thought that we can grow beyond where we are now in any area of our lives purely through our own efforts. Although many of us would love to be musicians, few of us are born with the natural talent of a Beethoven or Handel. However, we can still be outstanding musicians simply by repeated effort-- practicing day after day, gradually advancing to higher and higher levels of aptitude. As I mentioned above, if we can strive to improve by one percent a day, this seemingly miniscule amount adds up over the weeks, months, and years. I've also heard it said that in order to truly master a craft, we must dedicate at least 10,000 hours to it. That's approximately ten years of consistent practice. How many of us could commit to putting in 10,000 hours into our craft in order to reach a level of mastery? I would say although all of us are capable of doing it given the right incentives and motivation, unfortunately few of us possess the follow-through to put in this amount of time. I mean, we have to watch TV, do the laundry, and pick up groceries, right? I'm being facetious, of course. While it is true all of us are given the same number of hours in a day, what we do with those hours is completely, for better or worse, up to us.

5. "Many of life's failures are people who did not realize how close they were to success when they gave up." -Thomas Edison

I've heard this idea expressed in several different ways over the years, but this quote from one of the most important and influential American scientists in history expresses the idea well. I was lucky growing up in the sense that, although we were poor by Western standards, my parents instilled in my siblings and me some very good values, one of which was the power of persistence and of never giving up. So whenever I hear about people giving up in the middle of a project or undertaking they started-- undoubtedly many times initially feeling very passionate about it-- I am truly astounded because I have a great deal of trouble relating to this. In other words, what would lead a person to give up mid-way on something they had started? Giving up in and of itself is bad enough, because as I've emphasized throughout this book, the only way to reach your given objective at any point in time is to focus your energy consistently upon it until you accomplish it. However, perhaps what's even worse is that when people give up, they are many times very close, in fact, to reaching their goal.

I previously mentioned the old stories about the oil driller who gives up drilling just a few feet short of hitting the oil reserve, or the stone mason who chisels away at the stone and gives up just a few taps away from cracking the stone open to reveal the treasure inside. These anecdotes and others like them express the thought Edison so eloquently articulates. Edison was certainly very qualified to speak on this topic, as he failed literally hundreds of times before he invented the light bulb. Imagine what would have happened had he given up just a few experiments away from hitting his mark. Where would the world be today? While it is true that another scientist may have eventually come up with something to help us illuminate our homes, schools, and businesses, it may not have been for another 20, 30, or even 40 years, thus very likely changing the course of modern history. Therefore, I challenge you not to give up before you reach your mark. You can never quite be sure just how close you are to reaching it.

6. **"Let me tell you the secret that has led me to my goal. My strength lies solely in my tenacity." - Louis Pasteur**

Again, this echoes several of the ideas already presented in this treatise as well as some of the other quotes I already shared with you (is it just coincidence that many of the great minds in history thought the same way?). Louis Pasteur was another of the most famous scientists in history and is given credit for the process of pasteurization that we all take for granted with the food we consume today. I consider it so interesting, and quite inspiring, that many of the greatest minds in history did not judge themselves exceptional-- they merely thought of themselves as persistent and tenacious. I take great comfort in this because, although I consider myself to have a great deal of common sense and "street smarts", I don't possess much formal education beyond high school (I attended community college on and off when I was much younger). Thus, to hear these kinds of quotes gives me great hope for what I am able to accomplish. Moreover, I deem it noteworthy that these same common themes appear repeatedly. Pasteur, although I'm sure a brilliant man, considered his greatest personality trait to be his tenacity. I imagine if you could talk to him today, he would tell you that he simply refused to give up.

7. **"Mistakes are the portals of discovery." - James Joyce**

This is an extremely inspiring quote because I know how many mistakes I've made over the years. In fact, sometimes it seems the more I have tried to "make things happen" with my business ventures, the more mistakes I have made! However, mistakes are not to be looked down upon or shunned. Have you ever heard the adage, "If you're not making mistakes you're not trying hard enough"? I think the idea behind this is if you're just "playing it safe" in life, not taking any risks, just allowing your life to unfold in front of you, you're not likely to make many major mistakes (although personally I think this type of life philosophy is wrong). However, if you're out there really trying to make things happen, you're very likely to make mistakes. James Joyce, the famous nineteenth century American poet, expressed an alternative paradigm about mistakes when he called them "the portals of discovery." In other words, mistakes will lead you to the next level of accomplishment and achievement, regardless of what your field of endeavor happens to be. Whenever I am frustrated with myself because of what I at that point consider a bad decision, I am reminded of this quote.

As I have also emphasized on many occasions throughout these pages, it is also comforting to know if the greatest minds in history made mistakes, then certainly I can be allowed to do so as well. I'm sure you've watched a movie or television program and thought to yourself, "Wow, that scene was perfect!" However, what we do not realize, what we are not privy to, is how many times the actors had to rehearse the scene before it came out perfect. Many times, it's five times, ten times, or more before the actors get things "just right." In real life, however, obviously we don't have this luxury. It's just a "one shot deal" on most occasions. Although mistakes are a part of life, what we can do is to change the way we think about mistakes and begin to embrace them-- use them as tools to help us to become our better selves.

8. "A ship in harbor is safe, but that is not what ships are built for." - William Shedd

This is another of my favorites-- it's quite inspiring to me because I feel encouraged to get out there, take risks, and "put it on the line." Sure, ships in harbor are kept in pristine condition and are "safe," but what good is that? Although it's nice to be attractive and kept in good order, I'd rather take the ship out and test it on "the open waters." It's similar to an off-road vehicle of some sort. Yes, it does look pretty after it has just been washed and waxed, but is that why you bought it? No, you bought it to take out to the mud pits or to the mountain slopes and to put its strength and prowess to the test.

In our own lives, it unquestionably feels safer when we're "in harbor," but when we're elderly and looking back upon our lives, will we be satisfied with ourselves for playing it safe? In fact, someone once told me about a useful tool called "the rocking chair test." It's very simple really-- when you are faced with a situation in which you are not sure about whether the risk is worth taking, imagine yourself at 80 or 90 years old and sitting in your rocking chair, looking back upon your life. Would you feel regret if you didn't do what it is you're considering at this moment? In other words, would you regret not approaching that person to whom you are attracted? Would you regret not taking those first steps toward opening your own business? I know in my own case, when I put something to the "rocking chair test" I am immediately motivated to take the action I'm considering. I don't know about you, but I tend to regret the things I didn't do more than the things I did do. So remember-- although a ship in harbor is safe, that is not why ships are built!

9. "When you cease to dream, you cease to live." - Malcolm S. Forbes

Ah, to dream. We all do it-- especially when we are young. Do dreams have to stop there, though? In my opinion, they surely do not-- and apparently, Malcolm Forbes, one of the great businessmen of the twentieth century and founder of Forbes magazine, felt the same way. Does this mean we will achieve every single one of our dreams? I'm certainly not going to tell you that you can't, but I know that I personally will never achieve all of mine. I just do not think I will have the time or energy to achieve each one-- but that does not keep me from trying. However, I think just the act of dreaming, of having goals, of thinking about possibilities, of imagining things you would someday like to do-- that's what keeps us alive and passionate about the days to come.

I remember when I was a little girl in Thailand, dreams of coming to America and being a movie star are what kept me going. Looking back on those times, I sometimes feel those were silly dreams-- I mean, after all, how many of us out there actually become movie stars?-- but that's what kept me going at that moment. I've heard stories about soldiers held in POW camps for years at a time. What do you think kept them going? It was dreams-- dreams of what they would do when they got home, dreams of a special girl they would end up marrying, dreams of that house in which they would raise a family. Regardless of whether they actually achieved those dreams-- although certainly some of them did achieve the dreams they envisioned-- the very act of dreaming, of picturing the life they wanted, gave them enough mental impetus to survive until the next hour or next day. There is infinite value in the very act of dreaming.

10. **"Go confidently in the direction of your dreams. Live the life you have imagined." - Henry David Thoreau**

There is something about the future that never ceases to inspire the human race. We as a species have always been optimistic about the road in front of us. Part of this innate optimism, in my opinion, rests in our ability to dream-- to imagine the future we desire for our families and ourselves and to pursue it. However, despite this innate quality that seems to be unique to humans, only a small fraction of humans over time have actually been able to achieve their dreams. Now granted, perhaps in the past this ability was more constrained by economic and technological factors. However, I would venture to say almost everyone alive today has the economic and technological resources to be able to place into reality the life he or she desires-- to create the future he or she imagines.

In my view, the bottleneck today for the vast majority of people is not the resources we have (or do not have) at our disposal-- it is the *courage* and *drive* to turn our dreams into reality. Most people have some sort of vision in their mind's eye of how they would like their futures to be-- whether it's to be an athlete, an entertainer, a doctor, a lawyer, a small business owner, or countless other options. However, only a fraction of us really even do anything at all to try to turn these visions into reality! Why is that? Is it because most people are just plain lazy? Although some folks might argue that's the case, I really don't believe it is. I believe all of us can be inspired to do great things given the proper incentives.

From my perspective, people don't achieve the life they desire for a couple of reasons. First, although people may intend to create the life they yearn for, they get caught up in the day-to-day routine of everyday life. You know, doing the laundry, cooking dinner, taking out the garbage, picking up the kids from soccer practice-- not to mention their 40-hour (or more) a week job needed to perpetuate all of this. Do you think the most successful people over the years didn't have these sorts of responsibilities? Of course they did. Nevertheless, they chose to make their dreams-- and the daily activities that would ultimately lead them to their dreams-- a priority. That is, they did these things before they did anything else-- they may have gotten up an hour or two earlier every day to work on them, or stayed up later, or focused on them on Friday and Saturday nights instead of going out with friends. Second, and there really is no way to "sugar coat" this, is it takes courage to follow your dreams-- courage we all potentially have, but very few of us can actually call forth and use.

Do you think the most courageous people throughout the course of history didn't feel any fear when they decided to undertake a risk? Of course they did-- whether a famous general leading his army into battle or a famous entrepreneur who quit her job to focus full-time on her invention or business idea. Are you familiar with the saying, "Feel the fear and do it anyway"? I think we all could be reminded of this simple inspirational thought from time to time. So take the words of Henry David Thoreau to heart-- go confidently, live the life you long for, and make those dreams into your reality.

11. **"There is a fountain of youth: It is your mind, your talents, the creativity you bring to your life and the lives of people you love. When you learn to tap this source, you will truly have defeated age." - Sophia Loren**

Isn't this what it is all about? To use the gifts that God has given us in order to touch other people's lives? I have always been a big fan of Sophia Loren. As a young actress, she was one of the most beautiful and glamorous starlets on the Hollywood and international movie scene. Now well into her 70s, she continues to inspire millions of people around the world not only with her physical beauty, but also with her grace and inner beauty, as evidenced by the above quote. I believe when you cease to contribute, cease to grow as a person, and cease to set and achieve new goals for yourself, you slowly begin to die. If you truly want to stay young, you will continue to use those gifts you have been blessed with and constantly strive to develop new talents. This quote to me is truly inspiring.

12. **"The greatest danger for most of us is not that our aim is too high and that we miss it, but that it is too low and we reach it." - Michelangelo**

Michelangelo was perhaps the most gifted "Renaissance Man" of the fifteenth and sixteenth centuries. He was a sculptor and painter but was also gifted in many other areas as well. I chose this quote to share with you, and left it for last, because I wanted to give it its proper place among these other quotes. I feel while the first eleven are also excellent, if we were only to remember or take heed of one of the twelve, it should be this one. I know I have been guilty of "aiming too low" many times in my life, and I'm sure you could say the same thing as well. Of course, there many ways to interpret the above quote. One thing

Michelangelo is saying is we should never be afraid of failure if we truly have our sights set on a worthy goal or objective. It is much better, in his view, to "fail" at something after we have truly dared to dream big versus having been "successful" at something much below that which we are actually capable.

Again, as I've stated consistently throughout, we only have one life to live-- although that sounds trite and cliché, it's true. Aren't you curious as to what you can accomplish if you truly set out to do so? I know that I am. I feel while on some level I seem to be successful, there are so many things I still want to do and feel capable of doing.

I'd like to leave you with one final thought. As we've talked about, "failure" is nothing more than a state of mind, something you experience internally. If you do not acknowledge failure, does it really exist? You recognize by now that every person who ever achieved anything in the history of this world failed hundreds, if not thousands, of times before becoming what everyone else considered "an overnight success." If you remember nothing else, please remember to set your sights high and don't be afraid to go after what you really want.

Chapter IX
The Plan: What Do You Want to Accomplish?

Over the course of this book, we have been on an incredible journey together-- traveling from one of the poorest regions of the world to the pinnacle of what many would consider the "American Dream." My hope is that you have seen how someone who by the laws of probability would have little chance of ever being successful *can* make it in the "Land of Opportunity." I truly feel blessed for everything that has occurred on my voyage through life. My goal in this chapter is to tie together all that we have learned so you may start to use these things immediately and effectively.

What have we learned over the course of this journey? The first thing I want to emphasize is to *think big*. Regardless of where you are now in your life, your mind can envision where you someday aspire to be. The mind is an incredible tool-- scientists don't fully understand its power and don't really know how thoughts affect reality. However, I can tell you, along with millions of others who have experienced the mind's power, that thoughts certainly do have an impact in the physical world. Isn't it to our benefit, even if we do not understand exactly how it works, to utilize the mind's power of thought to create our own physical reality-- the reality that we desire for ourselves?

It's like the incredible phenomenon of electricity. How many of us could actually explain in any sort of detail just how electricity works? I speculate that very few of us could; however, this doesn't stop us from using it on a daily basis. Recently, studies on the science of thought have emerged whereby scientists place subjects in an MRI scanner to detect what physical energy is emitted via thoughts. From the basis of the MRI results, it is quite clear that thoughts do indeed emit energy and are organic impulses. Therefore, it's really not much of a stretch to assume that thoughts do contain some sort of power to influence the physical world. Therefore, the bottom line is that I encourage you to think big.

Although the previously described step is essential, we also have to get clear on what it is that we want. You remember our SMART acronym as it relates to goals, don't you? Can you recall New Year's resolutions that you, your friends, family, and coworkers have made? What are the typical resolutions? If they're anything like the ones I'm familiar with, they are things like, "to lose weight", "to make more money" or "to be more attractive." Although objectives like these are better than having no aspirations at all, what's wrong with goals like these? They're too vague! What does "to make more money" mean exactly? In theory, it's a great goal-- I mean, who doesn't want to earn more money? However, as a specific goal, it is far from optimal.

I discovered something a long time ago that is essential to reaching a goal. Although a vague goal is better than no goal at all, it's exponentially more effective to have a *specific* goal-- something you can quantify to ensure that you're actually reaching it. For example, why is the specific goal of "to lose ten pounds" so much better than "to lose weight"? Well, I'm not a psychologist, so I couldn't tell you what it is in the mind that makes the former so much more effective, but "to lose ten pounds" is something you can measure each day, or even twice a day if you so choose! In an instant, you will know if you are getting closer or farther away from your goal. There's instant feedback. It's also something you can track on a day-to-day basis. Here's how to make a specific goal even better-- put a timeline on it. In other words, give the goal a deadline. So now, we have the goal of "to lose ten pounds by April 1." This is a great goal-- it's specific, measurable, and has a timeline. Thus, as each day passes and your timeline slowly elapses, you know if you are on track or not.

Now that we're thinking big, and are clear on what we want, what comes next? The next thing is to plan a *strategy* on how we will achieve what we want. For example, we know we want to lose ten pounds by April 1. That's fine, but now how exactly do we do that? Are we going to walk every day for 30 minutes, lift weights three times a week, swim every other day for an hour, or some combination thereof? Obviously, any sort of exercise would help, but it would be to our advantage to have a firm plan of attack, a strategy as to how we will lose this weight-- a formal workout regime, if you will. It would also be beneficial to include or exclude items in a methodical, deliberate manner-- not simply, "oh, I think I'll just ride my bike three times a week." Educate yourself as to the different forms of exercise, how they will help your body, and what you can expect from each form of exercise. Now you can approach your workout regime in a confident manner-- you have methodically chosen the exercise and/or diet strategy that will most effectively help you to lose weight. Again, your goal could be anything. Just get clear on exactly what you want and plan a strategy on how you will achieve it.

Have you ever heard the metaphor, "Life is a journey"? Although this seems like a much-overused cliché, I believe it contains a wealth of truth. In my opinion, a corollary to this is the question of, "Is there a final destination?" In other words, are we pushing through life, making goals and plans and forging dreams, in order to "arrive" somewhere we can finally say, "I made it"? For example, I know many people-- myself included—who are guilty of thinking about retirement in this way. In other words, many people out there go to work day after day, month after month, year after year with nothing more to drive them than a vague notion that someday they would be able to retire. However, people's ideas of "retirement" are drastically different.

Actually, the concept of retirement is rather new-- it's only been around since the first part of the twentieth century. Before then people simply worked right up until the point of passing on. However, beginning around the time of the Great Depression, in the 1930s, with the implementation of Social Security, people began to think about retirement in its current form. However, even at that time, people could not expect to live much beyond age 65, so retirement and Social Security were only designed for the last few years of someone's life. However, today, the term "retirement" is much more ambiguous-- what does it truly mean? Does it mean that a recently retired person, someone who has been active all of his or her life, will now just putter around the house, tinker with things in the garage, or spend almost all his or her waking hours in the garden or on the golf course?

As you are probably aware, people are living much longer than ever before. In fact, the fastest demographic group is the centenarians-- those who live to age 100 or more. So what is a person to do with 30 years or more of "retirement"? I couldn't imagine this type of sedentary lifestyle for decades and believe most folks would concur with me. In fact, many people, after an entire adulthood of hard work and pursuing achievement with nothing more than a vague notion of retirement to look forward to, end up actually dying after a few short months or years in this form of sedentary lifestyle. I think it's tough mentally, spiritually and physically to make such a radical shift in one's whole essence of being.

Therefore, when we arrive at this age, it's essential to have a firm, clear set of goals for this stage of your life. If planned properly, these years are truly something to look forward to and to be thoroughly enjoyed. If money is not an issue, that's wonderful. If it is still an issue, that is all right as well-- you just have more limited options. What do you hope to accomplish during these years? Would you want to travel, perform volunteer work or something along those lines? These are worthwhile endeavors, but it's probably to our benefit to put as much thought into this phase of our lives as we did in the other phases of our lives, such as our career phase.

With that said, let's go back to the notion of life being "a journey and not a destination." Let us think about this for a minute and what it is in fact trying to convey. Although certainly a change of mindset for many of us, I believe this is communicating that we should live each day in the present and to enjoy the gifts that each day offers. If we don't, and are simply focused on the future, some amorphous end destination, then we may overlook the present, which, as we all know, is the only thing that we are promised. Does this seem like a contradiction from all the things we have been discussing relating to goals and knowing what we want in life? I think at first glance it might, but there is a way to resolve these two seemingly disparate ideas. I believe while we should have clear goals and know where we want to go in life, it is also important to be mindful of the present and not just live for what we hope to achieve at some point in the future. In other words, let us not get so hung up on the future and achieving our long-term goals that we completely forego happiness and current satisfaction with our lives and not give ourselves the right to feel good about where we are now. As we all know, many tragedies occur every day across the globe to people who have goals, feel hopeful about the future, and have things to look forward to in life. Therefore, my challenge to you is to take the time to create your future, but not at the expense of forsaking the present.

You now have the knowledge and tools to make your life the way you want it to be. I believe we all have things we want to do in life and that we are certainly able to accomplish if we align our priorities and mental, physical and spiritual faculties. If you take nothing else from this book, I would like you to take away the power of goal setting-- of actively designing your life around those things, experiences and states of being that you deem truly important to you. The thoughts you think, the internal dialogue you have, and the habits you perform on a daily basis all help ultimately to shape your destiny.

I encourage you not to let your learning and quest for personal improvement end here. Make a vow to yourself to continue your learning-- continue to fill your mind with good information, positive thoughts, and role models who have achieved what you want to accomplish. Shun those people who try to tear down your dreams, whatever they happen to be. Your mind is like your body in that it needs to receive continual nourishment in the form of learning and reinforcement of things you wish to come through and manifest themselves in the physical world. Again, take at least 30 minutes a day to read, listen to a book on CD, or otherwise provide uplifting material for your mind.

Also, remember your mind and spirit are like your muscles in the sense that you must exercise them on a consistent basis to keep them strong. It's not sufficient to read for 30 minutes one afternoon and then say, "Oh, now I'm set for life." You wouldn't exercise for 30 minutes and then think you were set in that area for the rest of your life, would you? The same can be said for your mind/spirit connection. Thus, commit yourself to a lifetime of learning and constant improvement.

I would also ask you to take some time to discover what you are truly passionate about. There are too many distractions to throw you off-course otherwise. Although I *liked* what I did for those years working in civil service, I wasn't *passionate* about it. It wasn't until I began to branch out, first with real estate and then with the jewelry store, that I began to be passionate about what I did. If you look at the most successful people, which happen to be the ones who earn the most money (is this simply a coincidence?), they are the ones who are passionate about what they do in life. In other words, they would do what they do for free. In many cases, they did do it without being paid for many years-- such as those in the entertainment industry or professional athletes. In fact, one of the first things many of these people say when they finally do receive a salary-- which at that point is usually quite large-- is, "I can't believe they're paying me for this!" I mean, isn't life enough of a drudgery? Why do something unless you are excited about it?

If you are not quite sure what your passion is yet-- and granted, they tend to change and evolve over the years-- go to the library or bookstore and examine some books on the subject. There are a number of good ones out there, such as the classic *What Color is Your Parachute?*, which is considered the "job hunter's bible" and is updated yearly. Now you might be thinking, "But I'm not really looking for a new job." I respect that; however, it does have many different exercises that lead you into some deep thought about your interests, proficiencies, what you've done in the past that has qualities and characteristics of "potential passions," etc. In addition, the internet is full of websites with personality and other related tests that will help you to bring out those qualities you didn't even realize you have. They will help you to analyze those broad, overarching personality traits that could apply to different careers. Many times, they will even provide you suggestions of careers that might be well suited for you. I have actually done these kinds of tests, and have gone through the exercises in the book mentioned above, and

I can honestly say that they are worth the time and effort. In my case, they were spot-on accurate and helped me years ago to begin thinking about self-employment, and more recently, reinforced the decisions that I'd made regarding having my own business.

Entrepreneurship is a wonderful career path-- and I believe it could be considered a legitimate career path like any other-- but it's not for everyone, at least in the traditional sense. If you don't think you're ready or able to drop everything and set your sights on becoming a full-time business owner, start small. In other words, perhaps look into a home-based business while keeping your full-time job. A large percentage of successful business operators started this way. However, there are many frauds out there regarding home-based businesses, so be careful and do your research first. For some ideas regarding potential . (legitimate) endeavors, consult such publications as *Entrepreneur* magazine or one of the many other similar periodicals-- although personally I prefer this one. This way you can have the best of both worlds-- the security of your full-time, salaried job with the excitement of your new venture. Of course, at some point, if your undertaking grows beyond a certain point, you would need to make a decision as to which direction to go.

If there's one thing I would like you to get out of this book, it's to be true to yourself-- take the time to discover what you want to do and make a plan towards its accomplishment. In my mind, having a *written plan* for the attainment of specific goals is perhaps the highest value-added activity there is as far as self-improvement goes. However, unfortunately, it's also something very few of us actually do. Many people get very excited about making improvements in their lives and have the energy and motivation to succeed. However, the majority simply do not take the time to make specific goals and then, just as importantly, go that one crucial step further and develop solid plans for the realization of their goals.

Chapter X
Final Success Strategies

I would like to sum up this book with my final thoughts on life success. These items are distilled from the knowledge I have picked up in my personal and professional life as a struggling immigrant, civil servant, and then successful entrepreneur. This is a synthesis of my life's successes, failures, and learning experiences. My hope is that you will take these and use them to help evaluate your own life.

1. *Do the best you can in all endeavors, but then "let the chips fall where they may."* Although I've mentioned it before, I want to reiterate the *One Percent Rule*. You will make unbelievable progress in any area of your life-- whether it is trying to learn a new language, a musical instrument, or studying for your MBA-- if you try to improve just by one percent a day. The idea is that although this amount of improvement seems miniscule, after relatively little time has passed, the results can be truly inspiring. What's more, a one percent improvement a day in your area of concentration is not that difficult to achieve. It's really just a matter of focus and making something a habit. However, imagine you improve one percent a day for week after week, month after month. The results begin to compound and before long, you have doubled your ability in that area, and then doubled it

again. I've tried to follow this advice over my life, and I can attest to the power of this principle. In fact, it's very similar to my approach in writing this book. My goal since starting my writing has been to write one page a day. This does not seem like much, but think about it-- that's 30 pages a month, 90 pages in three months, etc.

However, sometimes, regardless of how hard we push ourselves and give it everything we have to achieve the goal, things still don't work out. In my view, this is because there are so many outside factors that are beyond our control that we many times don't foresee. Examples include coming down with a serious illness, having an accident, having a child with a serious problem, etc. Additionally, we can't control the actions of others.

In the business world, for example, we may think we have a wonderful product that will be a surefire bestseller. However, perhaps due to conditions in the economy, or what marketers predict consumer demand to be over the next couple of years, we may never be able to launch the product or have to wait much longer than we had first anticipated. Therefore, it behooves us to remember in today's complex world, there are hundreds of other factors beyond our control that can potentially influence our short-term success. This doesn't mean we will never become successful with whatever it is-- that's where persistence comes into play. However, it does mean we need to remember simply to do our best, and "let the chips fall where they may." Put another way, we should always strive to do our best and then trust that things will work, either now or in the end. Remember this is what faith is all about.

2. *Money comes and goes, but experiences and memories stay with you forever.* I'm the first one to admit that in today's world, money is an absolute must. We must have it to survive on a daily basis. No matter how frugal we are with our spending, we have to pay our mortgage, buy groceries, clothes, etc. There are thousands of books devoted exclusively to the subject of money and how we can better manage it, change the way we feel about it, etc. so I won't spend time delving into this area. If you are interested in the study of personal finance and money in general, I encourage you to go to the local bookstore or library and spend some time reading. In fact, many bookstores will permit you to sit down and read some of the books they have on their shelves.

However, I would also emphasize that although money is essential, it is not the only thing in life. When I look back upon my life, I don't think about how much money I had or didn't have at any particular point. Instead, I think about the people I met, the experiences I had, and the memories I created. In other words, to me money is like the motor oil in the engine of your vehicle-- it's necessary, but it's really only the means to an end, not the ultimate experience you're wishing for. I have had the good fortune of being able to create many wonderful experiences, and I'm confident that when I am on my deathbed, I will look back on those experiences and feel thankful, blessed, and ready to go to the great beyond. Moreover, I am also certain money will not even enter into my consciousness at that point. Have money be your servant-- do not be a servant to it.

In sum, life is about experiences. Money is a tool, not the ultimate objective. Use money to help you enjoy the life you want. Money comes and goes. It's nice to know that even though we may lose money-- I've lost my fair share over the years- we can always find ways to get it back. Put another way, money is just energy. We need it to survive, but it's not what we're ultimately after. We as humans are designed to seek out relationships, experiences, joy, happiness, and life memories. Again, force money to be your servant-- not the other way around.

3. *Document your life.* Speaking of looking back on your experiences and life memories, be sure to document them through photography, writing, and other ways of leaving your mark and possibly sharing your life wisdom with those who follow us. I have always been fascinated by photography and developed an interest in it at a rather early age. I remember seeing photography books and marveling at the photos I saw in them-- of nature, people during important events, joyous moments, tragic moments, etc. It never ceased to amaze me how those photos would capture that moment in time forever. Over the years, I have tried to take pictures, and I have been good at keeping my personal photos protected for future enjoyment. In my early 20s, I was in the

Philippines with my husband during one of his military assignments. I participated in many of the on-base social events and was lucky enough to have a camera with me on many occasions or was with someone who had one. I have those photographs with me in albums and always feel a surge of pleasure whenever I reminisce over them.

Moreover, the act of writing is an ancient art that has captured people's imaginations for thousands of years. Although I have never kept a diary of any sort, I know people who have kept journals for years and feel inspired whenever they look back on them. In them, they normally have not only the daily events that happened to them over the years, but thoughts, ideas, stories of people they met and relationships they had, etc. Some of the most creative, well-loved, and well-respected artists, inventors and heroes throughout human history have kept written records of their lives-- people like Leonardo da Vinci, Napoleon, and Einstein. Imagine if you could read some of their journals! It's truly remarkable to ponder the very notion-- to have access to these people's ideas and innermost thoughts.

The other remarkable thing you can experience is to pull out your own personal notebooks from three, five, or ten years ago and go back and read them. You invariably will experience a sort of "so that's where I was" moment-- it's surreal to go back and read these things. This is especially true when you read your thoughts from periods in which many life-changing events were happening. The more detailed you are in your writing, of course, the more you will be able to relive those experiences. Many times you have to sit down because of all the emotion it conjures up. It's as if you stepped back in time.

4. *Remember to laugh as much as you can every day.* I've learned you can be just as happy as you want to be or just as miserable as you allow yourself to be. Our minds are like cameras. We can't focus on everything that happens around us at all times-- we have to "zoom in" on a portion of our surroundings at any given moment. Therefore, we only focus in on one particular "scene" of what is actually happening, meaning that our minds are inherently biased in that regard. If this is the case, why not use this to our advantage? In other words, why not try to focus in on the funny, humorous parts of situations instead of the negative parts?

Have you ever heard the proverb, "Laughter is the best medicine"? I've read a great deal lately about how laugher releases all kinds of feel-good chemicals in your body and actually does help your body to heal itself (remember the story of Norman Cousins?). With all the evidence in its favor, why not try to use this to our advantage and laugh as much as possible every day? Now granted, some situations-- such as a terrible tragedy of some sort-- are not laughing matters, but the vast majority of what you and I experience in any given day is nowhere near that serious. In other words, most of what we experience in our daily lives can be laughed at. Also, be sure to always possess a sense of humor about the world around us-- watch funny shows, talk with people who you find to have a sense of humor, and try to further develop that sense yourself.

5. *It's wonderful to have friends, but even better to be your own friend.* I have had some wonderful friends over the years. Some of my best friends have been other Thai nationals who came to the U.S. around the same time I did. I have always tried to be open to making new friends along the way, including friends in the military or civil service when I worked in that area or other self-employed individuals over the last few years. Studies show people with many friends live longer, happier lives, and I would definitely agree with that from my experience over the years.

Think about older people in our society. Some seem to be very content while others seem to be miserable and just surviving from day to day. Although physical health certainly plays a major role in this, it seems friendships and maintaining social ties are important elements of happiness at that age. Many times nowadays, with the advent of social media, retirees are able to rekindle old friendships and create other communal bonds, which I think is a wonderful thing to do on several different levels.

It seems when we are children and teenagers, we instinctively know the value of friendship, actively seek it out, and seem to be able to make friends very easily. However, when we get into adulthood we appear to lose touch with this part of our lives. Part of this may be expected, perhaps, as most of us get married, start families, and concentrate on getting our careers going. I've heard many people in their 30s and 40s remark that their spouse is their only friend. Although that is nice in a way, I believe we need other friends besides

our spouses to help keep us balanced and in-touch with the world. Therefore, the bottom line is that friendship is extremely important.

However, it is imperative to realize that you must be your own friend as well. This, in my opinion, is perhaps even more important over the long-term than having other friends. Let's face it-- in today's society, friends come and go. I have had very close friends over the years I haven't spoken to for ages. That doesn't mean they aren't important and that we couldn't potentially rekindle the friendship, but people change, evolve, move from one geographic location to another, etc. However, if we are our *own* friend, this in my view satisfies a great deal of this innate psychological need for companionship. Of course we should seek out other connections, but if we don't like ourselves, if we don't enjoy our own company, if we can't stand to simply be by ourselves from time to time to think, write, meditate, watch a funny movie, etc. then we will inevitably feel very lonely throughout a good portion of our lives.

I have known people-- and I have occasionally felt like this as well-- that simply cannot stand to be by themselves for more than a few minutes. Think about how much psychological pressure it is to feel like you must be with others at all times, not to mention how emotionally needy you might appear to others. So get to know yourself, what makes you "you," your thoughts, and your innermost personality. Because when it comes down to it, if we can't be our own friend, we're shortchanging ourselves.

6. *Never be afraid to reinvent yourself.* When you think of the pop singer Madonna, what comes to mind? Although I have always enjoyed her music, the characteristic that stands out the most in my mind is her tremendous ability to reinvent herself consistently over the years. She is one of the most successful recording and performance artists of all time, regardless of music genre. She has been making hit records and selling out shows for over 25 years. How is that possible? If you know anything about her, you will undoubtedly recall her many varied looks over the years-- from the *Like a Virgin* days of the mid-80s, the sleek *Vogue* look of the early-90s, and then into her more recent years as not only one of the few pop stars over the age of 50, but also a very successful entrepreneur. I'm sure she has realized that in order to stay viable as a force in the entertainment industry, she would have to continue to reinvent her musical style, appearance, and way of relating to the public. Regardless of whether you like her as an artist-- she's certainly been controversial enough over the years-- you

cannot deny the fact she is an entertainment genius and a master at staying relevant.

I believe we could all take a page from Madonna's playbook in this regard. I believe we must constantly strive to update our skills, learn new skills, and not be afraid of change. As fast as the world is transforming itself these days, we cannot sit back and think that whatever we did in order to be successful yesterday (or last month, or last year) will necessarily work today. We have to embrace change and not dread it. Change will always be there, and it seems to be happening faster now than ever before.

What does this mean for us? Well, for me personally, it means to read the small business magazines, attend trade shows, etc. to constantly be on the lookout for new trends in the world of commerce in general and the jewelry industry in particular. Since I am based in one of the premier tourist and conference destinations in the country, I also try to stay current with the latest developments in San Antonio and along the Riverwalk. You will need to examine your particular field to determine what the best way is for you to stay relevant and current. Perhaps not surprisingly, the need to be able to reinvent oneself is so pervasive in today's society and modern economy that the demand for adult education-- in both four-year colleges and technical schools-- is at an all-time high.

To figure out how to stay relevant over the years will require some thought and planning-- it's not something one can do "by the seat of one's pants." Do you think Madonna just happened to transform herself like that over the past three decades? Of course not. So I would encourage you to give this kind of thing some serious thought and deliberation-- again, this is a great thing to use a personal journal for. Let's embrace change and welcome it with open arms.

7. *Role models are inspirational, but remember that they are human too.* Since I was a little girl in Thailand, I have had role models-- people who I admired. When I was eight or nine years old, I looked up to my older siblings, especially my brothers. When I came to the U.S. as a teenager, my role models were the female characters portrayed in such television shows as "Wonder Woman" and "Charlie's Angels." Now as a more mature woman and business owner, I look up to other entrepreneurs, especially those who have made it big-- people like Bill Gates and Donald Trump. I have also had other role models at different points in my life, such as people I worked with as a civil servant-- perhaps a military officer I may have worked for, etc.

When emulating someone over the years, I have always attempted-- many times unconsciously-- to take some type of character trait I admired from the individual and make it my own. I think this is something most of us have done at some point in our lives-- in my view, it is a healthy, productive practice to engage in. We can even accelerate this process by reading biographies and autobiographies on people we admire-- people we may never meet (either because they lived in a different time or are otherwise removed from us) and would otherwise miss having access to. The lives of successful people have always fascinated me. We have so many books at our disposal that if we search, we will never be at a loss for a role model-- although we may never physically encounter that person.

In addition to these inspirational figures from Hollywood, sports or other walks of life who we will likely never meet, I believe it is a good idea for us to have friends who will motivate and encourage us to be better and reach beyond our present selves. In other words, attempt only to befriend or spend time with people who will pull you up, not drag you down. Since I came to this realization several years ago, I have made a conscious effort to associate only with people I believe are able to move me, encourage me, or otherwise elevate me to a higher place. When you stop to think about it, why would you want to associate with people who bring you down? In my view, many "false friends" out there receive a warped sense of satisfaction if they are able to drag you down. However, once you realize these people are in fact not your friends, it's easy to recognize the pattern and "nip it in the bud." Look for people who will inspire you-- to put it bluntly, life is too short to associate with losers.

Nevertheless, when we have identified individuals we want to emulate, we must be careful not to put these people on too much of a pedestal. It never ceases to surprise me how people can seem so distraught, surprised, and disappointed when a "role model" such as a professional athlete or entertainer lands in the news due to an infraction with the law. Notice that I put "role model" in quotation marks because in my opinion, these types of people are not individuals we should try to imitate. Regardless of who our personal heroes are, we must remember they too are human- - prone to the same temptations, vices, and bad judgment as anyone else. They make mistakes every day, just as we do. If you stop to think about it, though, this fact can also serve as a source of inspiration to us. That is to say, if our role models make mistakes and still have gotten to a point we also are striving to reach, this should take some of the pressure off-- in other words, we don't have to be *perfect*. In my view, that's a cause for celebration.

8. *We will all make mistakes; the important thing is to learn from them.* I have always believed in trying to improve myself throughout my life. When I was younger, like I mentioned earlier, I looked up to older family members. Now successful entrepreneurs and others who have done well in business serve as sources of motivation. However, I have found that no matter how hard I try, and despite my best efforts, I still make mistakes. Many times, I look back upon a mistake or something I would otherwise have done differently and think, "Why in the world did I do that?" Mistakes can be very discouraging if you allow them to be. However, once we realize we actually have control over how

we feel about and relate to mistakes, I believe this can greatly empower us.

Think about actors on the set of a television show or movie. When we watch a show or movie, it seems everything is perfect-- the lines, the movements, the choreography. Of course, the actors follow a script, or thorough set of directions, detailing what they should say, how they should move, even the facial expressions and body language they should put forth. However, despite all this, they still get things wrong a good portion of the time! I know you've seen bloopers from a TV show or movie-- sometimes it takes them three, four or even five times to get a line right! In fact, if you think about the word "mistake" from an acting standpoint, you could actually break it down into two parts: *mis-take*. In other words, it is a "take" that didn't come out quite right. It can be comforting to know that some of the highest-paid people in the world require several times before they get their lines right. It's fine for us to feel like we can also have a "do over" when we need to.

However, it's also important for us to try to learn from our mistakes. I know that sounds trite and cliché, but it's true. Moreover, in order to learn from our mistakes, we have to be willing to first recognize that we made a mistake and then stop long enough to think about the mistake and how we could do things better next time. Again, this is another reason to have a personal journal or some other way to record your daily thoughts and triumphs. Remember that thoughts are fleeting-- here one second and gone the next. I believe we can learn a great deal from our mistakes if we take the time to write down what we learned and how we could possibly do things better. However, regardless of whether you choose to write things down, have the courage to recognize your mistake, stop long enough to ponder it, and try to glean some sort of knowledge from the experience. In this sense, even *mistakes* will be victories.

9. *Although we are not guaranteed a tomorrow, plan for one anyway.* I have known people who use the fact we're not guaranteed a tomorrow as a sort of excuse for not planning for or thinking about the future. It is certainly possible that we are killed tonight on the way home from work or die suddenly of a heart attack or cancer next year. However, if we take care of ourselves and use common sense safety approaches, chances are that we will be around for many years to come. It actually surprises me to hear people say this kind of thing, because for me it's very depressing to think I might not be around in a month or year. I want to live to be a very old woman! I don't know about you, but I certainly want to *plan* to reach old age. One portion of this line of thought I do agree with, however, is leaving a will of some sort, perhaps even a living will or living trust. I am not a lawyer and don't want to give out this type of legal advice, but if you are interested in forming something like this, there are many estate lawyers around. In it, you can specify how and to whom you would like to leave your possessions. In sum, I

would encourage you to prepare for the inevitability of death with the hope that this event would not occur for many years to come.

If you are planning to live a long time as I am, I believe this empowers you to a large degree and encourages you to take better care of your health. Have you ever heard the saying, "If I'd known I was going to live this long, I'd have taken better care of myself"? Although this is obviously tongue-in-cheek, I think the point is very clear. We don't realize when we're younger the damage we can do to our bodies by excessive drinking, smoking, staying up late, or eating the wrong kinds of foods because the effects generally don't show up until later in life. However, the best time to start to care for your physical body is when you are young-- that is, when you can begin to put the correct habits into place that will serve you for a lifetime. In addition, youth is the ideal time to begin building a strong financial foundation. We talked about the power of compound interest a bit earlier, but it bears repeating-- the optimal time to begin investing is when you are young because you have time on your side. Your money will have many more years to grow. You can allow the power of compound interest to do all the "heavy lifting" for you in your quest to plan for a stable financial future.

Of course we all know we are not guaranteed a tomorrow. We hear and read about tragedy every day. However, this tends to give us a distorted view of our actual chances of living to old age. If we take care of ourselves, use common sense in our approach to life and refrain from excessive risk taking, we can very confidently plan for a long life. However, what we make of that long life is entirely up to us.

10. *Believe in something higher than yourself.* Since the dawn of time, man has had an innate urge to believe in something higher than himself. Throughout history, people have worshipped the sun, the stars, and the ocean, among other things. Today there exist dozens of major organized religions and hundreds of smaller, tribal sorts of religions. It has amazed me over the last few years to watch the news broadcasts and read the papers about all the religious tensions in the world, with each faith claiming to be the "true" religion. Although these faiths may appear quite different on the surface, at the core of each is man's need to believe there is an afterlife-- a higher power or something greater than ourselves. In other words, man doesn't want to believe this is it-- that when we die, it's all over. I believe besides fulfilling this innate psychological need, it helps us to make sense of the world around us. We need to believe there is a greater plan to it all.

Besides fulfilling this innate need, it helps us in our day-to-day life to believe the work we do, the sacrifices we make and the people we help or receive help from all has a larger purpose in life-- like little pieces fitting into a larger puzzle. It even helps those in less developed parts of the world, as they struggle to feed their families, many not having access to any sort of modern health care or other things we in the developed world take for granted, to think there is a better life awaiting them after this one. I know that it has helped me immensely whenever I have experienced tragedy or an otherwise difficult period in my life to think that the event happened for a reason and there is a greater purpose to it all-- even if I cannot decipher what that might be at the moment.

I would encourage you, if you haven't already, to develop a sense that there is something greater out there. In fact, it's hard to deny there is a higher being out there when you stop and ponder the beauty and wonder that surrounds us on a day-to-day basis. To believe in something greater helps us to deal with the vicissitudes, trials and tribulations, pleasures, and sorrows of life. I'm not advocating any particular religion-- I am not particularly religious myself. However, I believe it's important to tap into that spiritual portion of ourselves we all possess-- that part of our inner being that connects us to all other living creatures, even those who have come before us and those that will come after us. Once we do this, I believe that life takes on a richer, fuller meaning.

I would like to conclude this tome by thanking you for accompanying me on this journey through my life. My sincere hope is that you have found something you can use and apply to your own life. I feel the simple fact that you have read the words I struggled to put to paper connects us in some special way. Although we may never meet in person, I feel our souls are connected and that we are kindred spirits. I would like to leave you with a traditional Irish blessing, one you may have heard before, but one I feel truly sums up my feelings and appreciation to you and the sentiment I have attempted to convey in this book. It is the following: **May the road rise to meet you, may the wind be always at your back, may the sun shine warm upon your face, the rains fall soft upon your fields and, until we meet again, may God hold you in the palm of His hand.**

ACKNOWLEDGEMENTS

I would like to give a special notation of gratitude to the following individuals and organizations:

To my family who believed in me all of these years. I love you all.

Henry, I want to thank you for supporting me throughout the years and for introducing me to the real me, the one who was destined to become successful. You are my inspiration.

I must give tremendous gratitude to my "angel investors." They are the people who believed in me and lent money to me over the years for my business endeavors. I would never have been able to get off the ground and finally realize success without your backing.

Thanking D.P. Janssen and Darrell is an absolute must, especially during the difficult time with my mother in the hospital. Thank you so much. You were my rock and support system and remain such true friends to this very day.

To Heidi my photographer-- thanks for making me look good!

My new assistant Joemar has been especially helpful with audio-visual activities.

Rose Zamora, I so greatly appreciate your ongoing legal advice. You never steer me wrong.

Without Anne E. I would have never learned about "The Millionaire Mind." You are the one who introduced me to the wealth mindset, and I would never have known how to invest my money had it not been for you.

Then there are all of those friends who have believed in me over the years. The ones who never doubted me and always knew I could become successful. I remained on course due to your faith in me and appreciate those close friendships I have acquired along my life's travels.

REFERENCES

Bolles, R. (2011). *What color is your parachute?* Ten Speed Press.

Cousins, N. (1979). *Anatomy of an illness as perceived by the patient: reflections on healing and regeneration.* New York: Norton.

Mears, T. (2011, January 8). Don't break the chain with New Year's goals. *Miami Herald.* Retrieved on February 4, 2011 from http:// www.miamiherald.com/2011/01/08/2003929/dont-break-the-chain-with-new.

Padmasambhava, Kongtrul, J., Kunsang, E., & Schmidt, M. (2004). *Light of wisdom, vol. 1.* North Atlantic Books.

Roosevelt, T. (1910, April 23). Citizenship in a republic. Speech at the Sorbonne, Paris.

Seneca. Moral letters to Lucilius. Letter 13. Retrieved on February 17, 2011 from http:// en.wikisource.org/wiki/Moral_letters_to_Lucilius/Letter_1 3.

Shane, S. (2004). *A general theory of entrepreneurship: the individual-opportunity nexus.* Edward Elgar Publishing.

www.enotes.com/shakespeare-quotes. Retrieved on March 12, 2011.

www.quotationsbook.com/quote/38942. Retrieved on March 15, 2011.

www.thinkexist.com/quotes/buddha. Retrieved on March 7, 2011.

www.thinkexist.com/quotation/the_human_race_has_only
_one_really_effective/156393.html. Retrieved on April 9,
2011.

ALSO BY THE SAME AUTHOR

Inspired by a true story, this tale of courage and determination is sure to lift your spirits and make you want to cheer. Be careful, though. Once you pick it up, you will not want to put it down!